# HOW TO STUDY

# how to study

**CLIFFORD T. MORGAN** *and* **JAMES DEESE**

*The Johns Hopkins University*

McGRAW-HILL BOOK COMPANY, INC.

*NEW YORK TORONTO LONDON* 1957

*Drawings by Bob Gill*

XIII
43110

THIS BOOK has been written mainly for the growing number of students who continue their studies beyond high school. It is for all who are studying or who plan to study, either full time or part time, in a college, university, engineering or technical school, or any other school of higher education.

The book is a practical guide in methods of studying. It presents specific instructions for planning and using study time, getting the most out of a textbook, outlining and taking notes, and preparing for and taking examinations. It also gives directions for dealing with special problems such as studying foreign languages, writing themes and reports, and solving mathematical problems. The program of study spelled out here is based on years of educational research and has been soundly tested on thousands of students. We know that it works.

Every year untold numbers of students are in academic trouble simply because they do not know the techniques of study. Some fail, others get discouraged and lose interest, and others go along frustrated and dissatisfied with their academic progress. Furthermore, even very capable students need to know more about studying effectively. You can make use of this book in two ways: in a regular course on how to study and to learn a good set of study habits by yourself.

Although it is never too late to improve your study skills (they are valuable in the workaday world as well as in school), it is hardly ever too early to begin. If you are a high-school student planning to continue your studies after high

# PREFACE

school, we urge you to read and master the techniques presented here. We think too that your parents should read the book so that they can give you a helping hand and understand better some of the academic problems you are up against.

Learning to study isn't easy. You'll have to work at it hard. We will do our best to show you what you can do to become a better student. But you'll have to do more than read the book hurriedly. You should work out the exercises you'll find in it, and do the other things it specifically tells you to. After that, you should keep the book handy and, as study problems arise, use it for reference. Look up the section that bears on your problem, and try especially hard to carry out the remedy it prescribes. It may take you months—and possibly years—to put into practice all the techniques for improvement you'll find here. But if you work at them, you will be richly rewarded.

CLIFFORD T. MORGAN
JAMES DEESE

# contents

IF YOU ARE studying in college, planning to go to college, taking night courses, or, in fact, acquiring any sort of formal education, this book will interest you. It's mostly about studying. The chances are that you don't know nearly as much about studying as you should, for very few students do.

Studying—learning—is an art and a skill. It is an art you must practice to become what you probably want to be, a college graduate. Being a college graduate doesn't mean much in itself (except possibly to some personnel directors), but it stands for a lot of extremely important things. And you can achieve most of these things only through the studying you do. Just working at studying, however, won't guarantee you success in college any more than chipping away at a block of stone will make you a sculptor. Like most things in this world, there are good, skillful, and efficient ways of studying and poor, clumsy, and wasteful ones. If you take a good look at your study habits, you will probably find that there are a lot of things you are doing very badly. The purpose of this book is to help you discover them and to show you how to improve. If it succeeds in doing that—and we believe it will—it should prove more valuable to you than any other book you use in college.

**Who may improve.** This book isn't just for the poor student. Everybody going to college, no matter how good he thinks he is, has a lot to learn about how to study. Hence even if you are already a good student, you'll find in this book a number of pointers that will enable you to do

# ONE

# SUCCESSFUL

# STUDYING

more good studying in less time than you've been doing in the past.

Surveys of the problems of college students show that ineffective study is one of the biggest and most persistent problems students have. One thing we know is that students who recognize poor studying as one of their problems can be helped. And by utilizing a really systematic approach to the problem of studying, you can find better ways of studying than any single student has ever devised. That is what this book will try to do: It is meant to describe the modern methods of study evolved through survey and research and to describe them in such a way that you can put them to use.

The good student as well as the poor student stands to benefit from improvement in the efficiency of study habits. The poor student feels the need more because he is on the verge of failing, but sometimes the good student can profit

## VALUE OF HOW-TO-STUDY PROGRAMS

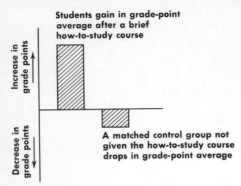

A comparison of average grades made by male students on probation at Stanford University after a brief how-to-study course and without such a course. (Based on S. L. Sharp, "Effective Study Methods," Journal of Higher Education, 14:271, 272, 1943.)

more by learning the proper techniques of study than poor students can. Many universities offer courses in how to study. At first they tended to give these courses only to students in difficulty. In time, however, they found that the best students could profit by the courses too, and they often were the ones who profited the most. You can see the results of one of these how-to-study programs in the accompanying graph.

So no matter how well you think you study, you can probably profit from this book. There is something in it that will pay dividends for you. If you are already making top grades, you can hardly raise your average; but, what is perhaps more important, you can achieve this level with more satisfaction and lasting value. If you have something less than top grades, you can obtain these benefits plus a pretty good chance of raising your grade average, especially in those subjects that give you the most trouble.

## THE ART OF STUDYING

Now what is studying? You may think it is what you do when you sit down with a textbook to prepare for the next class or examination. That is part of it, but only a small part. Studying is an all-out effort at learning, and it is only really

successful when you learn. To get a specific idea of all the things involved in effective study and of the shortcomings you may have, read and answer the questions in the inventory of study skills (How Good a Student Are You?). We'll run over the points in a general way in the paragraphs that follow.

**How efficient are you?**    The art of studying begins with the way you manage your life. A manufacturer wouldn't last very long if he waited until his employees ran out of materials before he bought new stock. Neither does the student manage very well by waiting to begin studying at the deadline for a paper or examination.

If you managed your personal finances the way a lot of students manage their studying, you'd soon be in hot water (perhaps you do; in which case, you probably *are* in hot water). If you don't save up part of your allowance or what you earn for your fixed necessities, you'll get in trouble. Of course, you might borrow money to get yourself out of trouble. But in education you can't borrow. Nobody can lend you a grade or the knowledge you should have gotten from a course by study.

In order to keep up in studying, you have to budget your time. You have to plan ahead for the day, the week, and even the term. When you get up in the morning, you have to have a pretty good idea of what you are going to do that day and then stick to it reasonably well. You have to do the same thing, looking further ahead, for the bigger items in the educational schedule, such as quizzes, examinations, and term papers. Without such a budget, you won't have the time you need to do the studying you are supposed to. Study skills won't do you much good if you haven't managed your affairs so that you can employ them.

How to budget time isn't just a matter of putting in so many hours a week studying or even of making sure to have work done on time. There are definite reasons for doing things at particular times: for studying German or chemistry at one hour of the day rather than another. We can't go into these reasons right here, but later we'll help you to devise a schedule, a budget, for your particular case and show you how to revise it in the light of your experience with it.

Besides budgeting, the art of study also involves a number of things you may not have taken too seriously: getting to class on time so that you don't miss the instructor's directions for studying and examinations, not cutting any more classes than you can help, finding a good place to study free of distractions, making sure to have good lighting, equipment, and other physical facilities for work, knowing when and where to ask the teacher questions about the work, regulating intrusions on your time and resisting temptations to postpone study, getting and following directions for the work entailed in each course, having the proper note-taking materials and keeping them well arranged and accessible. Some of these points may be obvious, some not. Even when you recognize that they are important, you may not succeed in doing what you should about them. Hence you may need help in actually doing the most obvious things.

To indicate just what they are, we are going

## HOW GOOD A STUDENT ARE YOU?

*Read carefully each of the following questions, and answer it honestly by writing a "yes" or "no" in the margin to the left of the question. When you are finished, see the directions for scoring at the end of the test.*

1. Can you think of anything that prevents you from doing your best work?
2. Do you usually study every day in the same place?
3. Do you usually know in the morning just how you are going to spend your day?
4. Does your desk have anything on it that might distract you from your work?
5. When studying, do you frequently skip the graphs or tables in your textbook?
6. Do you frequently make simple charts or diagrams to represent points in your reading?
7. When you find a word in your reading that you do not know, do you usually look it up in the dictionary?
8. Do you usually skim over a chapter before reading it in detail?
9. Do you usually glance through a chapter, looking at the paragraph headings, before reading it in detail?
10. Do you usually read the summary at the end of a chapter before reading the chapter?
11. Do you keep your notes for one subject all together?
12. Do you usually take your notes in lecture in outline form?
13. Do you usually take your notes on reading in outline form?
14. Do you usually try to summarize your readings in a sentence or short paragraph?
15. After you have read a chapter and taken notes on it, do you usually write a summary of the chapter as a whole?
16. Do you sit up studying late the night before an examination?
17. In preparing for an examination, do you try to memorize the text?
18. When you memorize something, do you usually do it all at one time?
19. Do you at times try to analyze your work to see just where you may be weak?
20. Do you often write an answer to a question and then realize that it seems to be the answer to some other question on the examination?
21. Do you consciously try to use facts you learn in one course to help you in your work on some other course?
22. Do you usually take notes in class just as rapidly as you can write?

*Some years ago Luella Cole Pressey gave questions like these to fifty good students and fifty poor ones at Ohio State University. Good students more often than poor ones answered them as follows: (1) no, (2) yes, (3) yes, (4) no, (5) no, (6) yes, (7) yes, (8) yes, (9) yes, (10) yes, (11) yes, (12) yes, (13) yes, (14) yes, (15) yes, (16) no, (17) no, (18) no, (19) yes, (20) no, (21) yes, (22) no.*

to ask a series of questions. Read each one carefully, ask it of yourself, and try to answer it. In this way you will be able to see what we are going to cover later and where you may be able to benefit from this book.

**How are your notes?**  Take the problem of keeping notes on classwork and reading. Do you take notes? Some students don't. What kind of notes do you take? Do you think they are adequate? Do you keep having the feeling that the instructor springs things on you in examinations that were not in the lectures or reading? If you do, it is probably because your notes are inadequate. Start out by thinking of all the things that are wrong with your notes and how you might improve them. You'll find some specific suggestions about this later on in Chapter Five.

**Can you read?**  "That's a stupid question," you say; "of course I can read." Indeed you can. But have you ever thought about how well you read? Some people read so poorly that, by comparison with people who read well, they are practically illiterate. Have you ever thought about how fast you read? How much faster could you read? (Nearly everybody can read faster than he does without special training in reading fast.) How much of what you read do you remember? (Most students don't remember more than half of what they read, even right after they have read it.) Can you decide what is worth trying to remember? Do you read charts and tables in a book? The captions for them? What do you do when you first start to read an assignment? What do you do when you finish reading the assignment? (Some students close the book and turn to something else.) How many times do you read an assignment? When? Do you read a textbook the same way you read a novel? Do you read chemistry and anthropology in the same way? If not, what's the difference?

**How do you prepare?**  Now, finally, let's raise some questions about your preparation for classes and examinations. Do you do assigned readings *before* or *after* you go to class? If you do readings before in some courses and not in others, which courses and why? Do you go to class with questions you would like answered? How often do you review your reading and your notes? When do you review? Do you review the same way for all subjects, or do you review differently for each course? Why? What does an essay examination test? An objective examination? How should you review for these different types of test? Do you run short of time in taking examinations? Why? Do you ever make foolish mistakes on examinations that cost you a lower grade? What are they? Why did you make them? Do the early examinations and quizzes in a course help you to prepare for, and do better on, later examinations? If not, why not? (They should.)

That's enough questions for the time being. The best student doesn't know the answer to all these questions, and when he thinks he does, he is often wrong. We're going to answer them all in this book—and more too, for these don't cover by any means all the items important in effective study.

**Basic skills.**  There is one general problem in studying effectively that we haven't mentioned. This is a deficiency in what we'll call "basic skills." These are skills that students are supposed to have mastered when they come to college but often haven't. One was implied above in the question about how fast you read. By any standard of what they could do, most college students are miserable readers. Not only do they read too slowly, they don't read the right way. They move their lips, retrace their words, and do other things that impede their comprehension of what they read as well as slow them down. This is something that's hard for us to remedy with a book, and it may require special training; but we can help the person who is only moderately handicapped by poor reading skills.

Another important skill has to do with vocabulary. Students aren't expected to know all the words they encounter in college, for learning the meaning of more technical and abstract words is part of acquiring a college education. And some teachers and textbook writers are unnecessarily addicted to long, complicated words and sentences. But some students, for one reason or another, haven't learned the precise meaning of words that all college students are supposed to know. You'd be surprised how often during an examination students come up to an instructor to ask the meaning of the most elementary (to the instructor) sort of word. Such students haven't been making the dictionary the bosom companion it ought to be. They're cripples hobbling through their classes and textbooks, missing the point of much of what they read and hear, merely because they don't really understand the words being used. You may be such a cripple, but fortunately something can be done to mend your verbal limp.

Simple arithmetic and elementary mathematics is a third skill in which all too many college students are deficient. The deficiency is especially serious for the student who undertakes a science curriculum, but it severely handicaps even the liberal-arts student. Many students can't solve correctly simple problems in multiplication and division, and an elementary algebraic equation like $y = a + bx$ freezes them in their tracks. This weakness is a serious handicap in college work. They may be able to get through history, French, or literature while being morons in mathematics, but they usually have at least one required course in the sciences. Moreover, many other subjects, such as psychology, political science, and economics, involve at least a little figuring with numbers and symbols. Even if they run the gauntlet of college courses without being downed by their poor mathematical skills, they'll have their troubles when they go into business or even when they try to manage their personal finances. This skill, then, is something students ought to assess and do something about if they are lacking in it.

We've tried to tell you in this section why nearly everybody who is now doing or planning to do college work needs to know more about how to study. We hope we have convinced you,

because we have found out from experience and from surveys of students that they do need to learn more about how to study. We know, furthermore, that almost all who need to improve their study habits actually can. Each person has his own combination of deficiencies, in budget management, specific techniques of study, or in basic skills. In subsequent chapters, we'll try to show you what you can do about them. In the meantime, we'll give some background for college work and consider the motivation for doing it.

## COLLEGE IS DIFFERENT

In high school, your fellow students probably represented a fair cross section of American young people. For that reason, the pace and standards of education were geared to the average student, not to the superior one, and the work you had to do was based on what could be expected of the average student. Like many people, you may have discovered that you could get by with very little work. Or even if you did work reasonably hard, competition wasn't so stiff and you didn't have to be particularly efficient about studying.

**Standards of work.**   Now what's the situation in college? Only about 30 per cent of students who finish high school go on to college. Though there are some exceptions, these tend to be the better high-school students. Certainly many more of the superior students than the poorer ones go on to college. Now you are in a faster league. All around you are students who were honor students, or at least very good students, in high school. You might have been the valedictorian of your high-school class, but there are usually dozens of valedictorians in a class of college freshmen. In college the pace and standards of education are geared to a superior group of students, not the average you knew in high school. The kind of work you used to do to merit an A or B can now easily get marked C, D, or even F.

Most students who go to college don't realize how much will be expected of them. Because many students don't gird themselves for a much tougher job of studying, they are disappointed and discouraged with their poor showing. This is why we believe this book is especially useful for the high-school student and the student entering college. If such a student can get a real idea of what is ahead and how to prepare for it, his chances of staying in college, liking it, and doing well will be enormously increased. You would be surprised how many students drop out of college without graduating. Many of these people are as able as those who make the grade, and in very many cases a little knowledge of the proper approach to study would have kept them in college.

**On your own now.**  Aside from competition and standards of work, there's another big difference between high school and college. In high school the work was pretty well laid out for you. Most of it was covered in class, and homework, which was easy for the superior student, could be done mostly in the one or

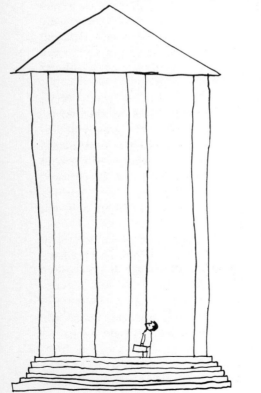

two periods set aside for study. You were graded to a large extent on what you did in class and on day-to-day homework. You might have had a few term papers and long-range assignments to do on your own, but for the most part you were paced by the daily round of classes.

All this is reversed in college. You spend relatively few hours in class, and except for laboratories and quiz sections, you are not graded very heavily on your participation in class. Instead of having an hour or two of homework for five or six hours of class, you now have two or three hours of outside work for every hour of class. There are no study periods in which you have little choice but to study. Instead, there are hours between classes that you can use profitably or waste away as you choose. On the whole, you are not required to do homework day by day and have it ready for the next class. Rather, you are given some assignments, and nobody checks on whether you did them or not for a week, a month, or even a whole college term. You may have an occasional quiz or hour exam, but in most courses whether you sink or swim depends on how you do in one, two, or three examinations.

What this all means is that you are suddenly thrown on your own. You are now treated like an adult who can be given some general directions and then left to figure out for himself how and when he will do what he is supposed to. This drastically different situation requires long-range, sustained motivation and wise budgeting of time. Many college students simply aren't prepared for this.

**Parental pressure.**  Making the abrupt change from high school to college is itself a big enough problem for the student, but this usually isn't all. There are plenty of other things to aggravate his problems. One of these, all too frequently, is the pressure put on him by his parents. There are all kinds of parents, nearly all of them well meaning, but some of them don't make the student's adjustment to college any easier.

For one thing, parents often don't understand

what we have just explained. They don't realize that the competition in college is keener, that the standard of work is higher, and that their children aren't adequately prepared for the change. They were proud of their offspring's being good students in high school. Being accustomed to seeing A's and B's on the report card, they may be pretty upset when their children's first college grades are several notches below that. At their kindest, they ask why their youngsters aren't doing better, whether they are trying as hard as they might, and so on. At their worst, they threaten to take them out of college if they aren't going to do any better than that.

Thus part of the trouble is that parents don't understand the difference between high school and college. For that reason, we suggest that they read this book to get a better idea of what their children are up against.

**Ability and interests.** There's another important point, too. Well-meaning but misguided parental ambition sends to college many youngsters who by ability and interests don't belong there. It is inevitable that some young people are not going to be interested in intellectual pursuits or in college life. They'd rather be mechanics, sailors, or farmers. There's nothing wrong with such interests, for society needs the kind of people who don't go to college as much as it needs college-trained people. Moreover, college-bred people have no corner on happiness or satisfaction in their work. The boy or girl who is really more interested in other pursuits than going to college should not be pressured into going.

Parents often don't understand either about the inheritance of mental ability. Some students don't have the mental equipment for college, and many of them are children of parents who went to college themselves or badly want their children to go. This eventuality should be no cause for blame or shame. It's simply one of the inescapable facts of life. It is a fact too that the students themselves must be prepared to accept. We're not saying this to discourage students but only to help them face their study problems more realistically.

**Overrating oneself.** In considering your prospects for success in college, there is still another point to keep in mind. Students, on the whole, are very poor judges of their own abilities and, indeed, of their own personal traits. Some overrate themselves, others underrate, but mostly they overrate. To prove this, we will cite one large-scale survey of whole classes of high-school and college students. Everyone in the class was asked to rate himself on each of a number of items such as speed of reading, vocabulary, note-taking ability, spelling, and grammar by putting himself into one of three groups: the top 20 per cent, the middle 60 per cent, the bottom 20 per cent. The ratings were anonymous; so the students had no one to fool but themselves. If they were good at rating themselves, you would expect their ratings to fall in about the same way, that is, 20 per cent top, 60 per cent middle, and 20 per cent bottom. But that isn't the way the results came out. Instead, only 1 to 8 per cent, depending on the item, put themselves in the bottom 20 per cent, but 35 to 60 per cent put themselves in the top 20 per cent. Obviously the students were unwilling to admit to themselves how deficient they might be in some traits, and they were inclined to see themselves through rose-colored glasses.

This, however, isn't true of everybody. Some people are fairly good judges of themselves, some grossly overrate, and some grossly underrate. In one study about 40 per cent placed themselves in the correct category, 40 per cent grossly overrated themselves, and 20 per cent underestimated their own abilities. (See the chart on the next page on which you can rate your own abilities and interests.)

What is one to do if he cannot rate correctly his own traits and abilities? Nowadays students are given many tests throughout the lower grades and, in many cases, upon entering college. When it is possible to learn one's score, it should be noted and evaluated. To do the evaluation, however, the student always has to consider the population which took the test, that is, the people he competed with. In high school, on an intelligence test, you might have scored at the 90th percentile, which means that you excelled 90 per cent of the students taking the test. However, this same score compared with that of students in college might be only at the 50th percentile. That is to say, 50 per cent of your college associates may do better than you did when only 10 per cent of your high-school associates did. It is therefore safer to learn, if possible, how your ability stacks up at your own college or the college you intend to go to.

To do this, the student may go to his high-school counselor or his college's counseling bureau, if there is one. Since the war more and more colleges have instituted bureaus or clinics where students can go for testing and advice on their college problems. In such bureaus, there are trained counselors who know not only how to give and interpret tests but also how to put together the whole picture of a student's academic and personal qualifications. Tests by themselves are far from infallible. (Partly for this reason, testing agencies often do not make known to students just how they did on a test.) Counselors know this, but they also know how to consider all sides of a student's problem and to help the student in a way that fits his individual case.

## SELF-RATING OF TRAITS AND ABILITIES

*In the spaces below, check where you honestly think you stand on the traits and abilities listed. After you have done that, discuss your ratings with some other people who know you really well—students, friends, parents, counselors—and who might show you where you have overestimated or underestimated yourself.*

**In my college, I think I am in the—**

| Upper fifth | Middle three-fifths | Lower fifth | |
|---|---|---|---|
| | | | in speed of reading textbooks |
| | | | in ability to understand textbooks |
| | | | in ability to take notes |
| | | | in general preparation for college |
| | | | in amount of time I study |
| | | | in not wasting time |
| | | | in work habits |
| | | | in vocabulary (words I know and use) |
| | | | in grammar and punctuation |
| | | | in spelling |
| | | | in mathematical skills |

## MOTIVATION FOR COLLEGE WORK

Motivation is the most serious problem facing many students. Often students don't seem to have any interest in their courses—or at least in some of their courses. They feel that they ought to be taking their college work more seriously. Very often students feel guilty about not studying, but they don't know how to work up the motivation for it. Lack of motivation is a deadly handicap to effective study. We can't give you motivation, but perhaps we can say some things that will help you develop some.

**Lack of motivation.** Why is motivation a problem with college students? Partly it's because of the vast difference between high school and college that we've already talked about. When someone is at you every day to do your work, hardly any internal push is required. All the motivation is applied from the outside. In college, these external pressures aren't so great, and you are left to move yourself to get your work done.

Another reason has to do with vocational aims. Most students who go to college express some sort of vocational aim. They want to be doctors, lawyers, engineers, salesmen, businessmen, and so on. These aims, though, are pretty vague, and they're shifting constantly. Few students are absolutely sure of what they want to be, and even fewer have any idea of what they must do in college to prepare themselves for their chosen vocation. Vocational counseling in high school and college is growing rapidly, and it will undoubtedly help many students to make up their minds a little earlier about what they want to be. Inevitably, though, many students will be vague and undecided. In fact, it is pretty hard for them to know what they are interested in and can hope to be until they have been in college for a while. Indeed, one of the things college should do for you is help you develop your aims. Even so, vocational choice is often difficult, especially in liberal-arts courses, which are fairly general and far removed from the practical problems of a vocation.

(See the list on the next page, which may help you organize your thinking on motivation.)

We can't do much in this kind of book to help you crystallize your vocational aims. Partly this is your own job, one that you must work out for yourself. Partly it takes time. If you are vacillating and uncertain and if counseling services are available, take advantage of them. The quicker you know what you want to do and what you can do, the faster you'll be able to settle down to college work with a real purpose. Having a definite purpose, you'll find it much easier to take on the habits and skills necessary for effective study and academic success.

**Academic and vocational success.** Even though deciding what you want to do is your job, we might help you out a little by pointing out some things that are true regardless of what you want to do. If, for example, you are interested in making a good income, look carefully at the following facts:

Those who make the best grades in college are generally those who make the best incomes later on. The member of Phi Beta Kappa, for example, typically earns considerably more than college graduates in general. And people who enjoy the distinction of being in *Who's Who* had, on the average, higher college grades than those who are not there. Many surveys of individuals in various groups have been made, and they all show a rather good correlation between grades in college and later success. For example, some years ago Walter Gifford, former president of the American Telephone and Telegraph Company, wrote an article in *Harper's Magazine* in which he pointed out that the earning capacity of employees in his company showed a very close relation to their grades in college.

There certainly are several reasons why this is the case: One, of course, is that those of the highest ability will usually succeed better both in college and in their work. You can't do much about native ability; so you needn't pay too much attention to this one. The other reasons, however, should provide some motivation for studying effectively. Employers are impressed by grades and offer better employment opportunities to those with higher grade averages.

Even more important, however—the same habits and skills that make for college success also promote success later on. In fact, the habits of work we teach in this book are not at all confined to college study. Almost all college-trained people are employed in positions where exactly the same skills are required. They must read rapidly while comprehending and remembering what they read. They must budget their time, much as a good student does. And they must "take examinations" almost daily when they answer the questions of their customers, employees, or associates. Their need for effective study habits is the same as that of the college student. Most people realize how important it is for them to be effective on the job, and

many of them wish that they had started earlier to acquire the proper habits and skills. This is the strongest reason we know of for acquiring good work habits in college before it is too late.

**Importance of grades.** If you entertain any idea at all of going on to professional school, what we're saying about grades is extremely important. In fact, it probably will decide whether or not you get into a law school, medical school, or graduate school. When you apply to such a school, you can be sure that your grades will be scrutinized very carefully because experience has proved that good grades are the best omen of success. Though a few people with "connections" may be admitted despite mediocre grades, this doesn't happen very often. Most graduate and professional

## MOTIVATION FOR COLLEGE

*The following questions are designed to help you think about your motivation and to give you some insight into it. Read completely through each group of items; then rank them in importance by using 1 for the phrase that applies best to you, 2 for the phrase that applies next best, and so on.*

I.  I came (or will go) to college because—

_____ I know what I want to be, and college preparation is necessary for it

_____ my folks wanted me to, even though I didn't

_____ I thought it would be a lot of fun

_____ I wanted to gain a better knowledge and understanding of the world I live in

_____ many of my friends did, and I wanted to be with them

_____ I wanted to get away from home

_____ I am particularly interested in athletics and student activities

_____ a college degree seems indispensable in this day and age

_____ I like to study and am particularly interested in certain subjects

II. I want to make grades that are good enough to—

_____ let me stay in college

_____ meet degree requirements

_____ let me participate in extracurricular activities

_____ put me on the honor list and give me

_____ special recognition

_____ make an outstanding record in college

III. My motivation for making grades is to—

_____ prove to myself that I am learning something

_____ secure a good job recommendation

_____ please my family

_____ do better than my competitors

_____ live up to my reputation of being a good student

_____ be respected by my teachers

IV. I sometimes don't study when I should because—

_____ I worry about my personal problems

_____ I simply can't get interested in certain subjects

_____ I am too involved in extracurricular activities

_____ I am bothered by illness and poor health

_____ I get distracted by things going on around me

_____ I tend to keep putting off my work

_____ I am easily tempted to do more interesting things

schools have two to ten times as many applicants as they can accept; they can afford to take only the best. In many fields, hardly anyone with less than a B average is considered for admission. Some schools can boast that they seldom admit anybody with less than an A or A— average. If therefore you are one who thinks he may want to go on to advanced studies after college, you ought to understand that your grades in college are all-important and work accordingly.

Grades, of course, aren't the sole measure of a man or of his academic success. Almost every teacher in public school or in college describes them as a necessary evil. They are only one somewhat imperfect measure of educational accomplishment. People can learn much and acquire a really useful education without having high grades, and some of the grinds who make straight A's may have concentrated so much on doing only what is necessary to make grades that they miss a valuable part of their education. On the whole, though, grades measure what one has learned, at least in courses, and what one can be expected to accomplish in the future. In fact, many scientific surveys prove that they predict as well or better than any other index the success of individuals in more advanced schooling and in the workaday world. So even though we may have some reservations about them, they are good things to work for and good things to get.

**Satisfaction in study.** Naturally, there are other reasons besides grades for being interested in improving your study techniques. Learning can be a lot of fun, and knowing what to learn and how to learn makes it even more fun. If you can pick up a book, read it quickly, know how to select the main points, and remember them, you're a lot richer person. Besides acquiring some useful and interesting information, you have a sense of satisfaction and the feeling of pride that a craftsman has in his handiwork. Though you can't see what you've done, you know you've accomplished something worth doing. Having done it once, you're in a better position to do it again. You

can read more and more and learn more and more. Learning then becomes an exciting and satisfying process, not a dull, frustrating experience. If you will apply yourself to developing the study methods described in this book, we can almost guarantee that you will come to enjoy studying and that you won't dread it the way so many students do.

**How to study less.** Another thought that might boost your motivation for learning how to study is this: Good study habits are mighty efficient; they let you get more done in less time. From the time you save, you have more left over for other things in college. You will be able to engage in more social and extracurricular activities or perhaps study things that are really interesting to you. If you're one who must earn part of his way through college, you'll have more time for such work without its interfering with your academic success. We can safely make these promises because they have been demonstrated. In many different universities, students who have been trained in how-to-study methods on the average make better grades with less time spent in studying than other students. Also consider two other facts that have been well proved:

First of all, it isn't *how much* you study as *how well* you study that counts. When students are divided into groups according to how much they study, it turns out that those who study a great deal, over thirty-five hours a week, say, actually make poorer grades than those who study less. This isn't necessarily because they have poor academic ability; every student knows somebody who seems relatively bright, who studies day and night, and yet for some reason doesn't get the grades he ought to. Educational psychologists who have surveyed students are pretty well convinced that the major factor is *quality* rather than quantity of study time. Though every case is different, the odds are that you too are one who could do more in less time if you only learned how.

**Part-time jobs.** Alongside this point we'll put another that may surprise you: College students

### DISTRIBUTION OF TIME SPENT IN STUDY

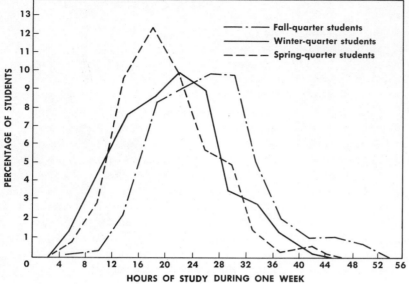

The curves show hours of studying each week for large numbers of students in a state university during the three quarters of the academic year. All the students were enrolled in how-to-study classes. Note the great variation in amount of study, some students studying as little as three or four hours a week and some as much as fifty-five hours a week. Also note the somewhat greater efforts of the fall-quarter students. (*After C. Bird and D. M. Bird, Learning More by Effective Study, Appleton - Century - Crofts, New York, 1945, p. 56.*)

who work earn on the average grades as good as, or better than, those who don't. In some cases, working students are distinctly better than the nonworking students.

There are probably several good reasons why the comparison turns out this way. Students who have to earn part of their way are likely to be more highly motivated than others. Paying some of their own bills probably makes it seem more important to them to get something for their efforts. Thus they try harder at their studies. Another reason may be that they are forced to budget their time more wisely than other students. Since part-time jobs usually have to be done on a schedule, working students must also study on a schedule or not get done. They can't afford to dribble away their

time. And the management of time, as we said before and will show in detail later, is an important facet of effective study. A final reason should be plain, even though it frequently isn't realized. There are so many hours in a week that there is plenty of time to work a few of them, enjoy many social activities, and still have lots of time for study—*if* the hours are used wisely. This brings us back to the point we started with: It isn't so much how many hours you study as how you use the ones you have. Except in very unusual circumstances, there is ample time to work, study, and play, assuming one knows how to do all three well. (It just *seems* as though there isn't!) And we'll prove it in the next chapter.

I**F YOU ARE** at all typical of the vast majority of students, you have at least one, if not more, of the following troubles: First, you don't get as much studying done as you should. Not that you don't try or even that you don't go through the motions of studying, but somehow or other you don't manage to accomplish as much as you know you should. Secondly, you waste time going from one thing to another. You try to study too many things the same day or evening or even within an hour. Hence you are so disorganized that you do not stay with one thing long enough to get something done. Finally, you have difficulty settling down to work. You are always getting ready to study, but for one reason or another, a lot of time goes by before you actually tackle a job.

All these troubles are slightly different aspects of the same thing. When you study, you just don't use your time and apply yourself so that you really accomplish something. Even if you're a student who thinks of himself as studying long and hard, the chances are that you are wasting time. In fact, if you study a lot more hours than other people, it's very likely that half or more of your time is being wasted.

## VALUE OF A SCHEDULE

Fortunately, these ills have remedies. The prescription, though, is not just one medicine but several. And they are all things you must do for yourself. Not all of them will work for you, but you must give them your best efforts until you have found the best combination for your individual habits and abilities.

# TWO

# GETTING

# WORK

# DONE

**A schedule saves time.** The first remedy—and this is something that is likely to be of use to everybody—is to set up a schedule for studying. A well-planned schedule makes time. It keeps you from vacillating about what you are going to do next. It sees to it that you are doing the right thing at the right time so that you aren't so helter-skelter about studying. It will cut out much of the waste motion in attempting to study. If properly managed, it assigns time where time is due, it keeps you from studying something more than it requires, and it lets you spend time where you really need it. With your time thus organized, you will find that you have more to devote to what needs it most and also more for things besides study.

**Making every hour count.** In the end, of course, you've got to make your own schedule so that it suits your class hours, laboratories, subjects, part-time work, and so on. We can only show you how to go about developing a good schedule. Let's start with the accompanying example. This is a schedule for a typical student carrying a fairly heavy load. He happens to be taking the following subjects: economics, psychology, German, organic chemistry, and English literature. Organic chemistry includes laboratory as well as lecture. The student who has this program is also employed ten hours a week, and his job calls for working two hours each weekday afternoon.

Notice first of all that the schedule is blocked off into one-hour periods. One reason for this is that many of the gaps in any student's class schedule are only an hour long. These hours add up, and only by using them can he keep from wasting a good part of his week. A more important reason, however, has to do with the psychology of work. Psychologists know from extensive research that people get their best work done by working intensively for a reasonable period of time, then resting or changing to something else. There is an optimum cycle of work and rest for every job and every individual. For the kind of work involved in studying and for the typical student, a period of forty or fifty minutes of work at a stretch followed by ten minutes or so of rest or change is just about right. Consequently, an hour used properly is pretty close to the best unit of time for most college study.

**When to study.** Notice too that the hours in the schedule are blocked off for specific subjects, not just for "study." That is partly to save the student time he might spend vacillating about what he is going to do and partly to ensure that he has with him all the needed materials for study. (Not being ready to study is one of the most common reasons for wasting time.) You can also see that, by scheduling hours for studying specific subjects, you can make sure you do your work in each subject as it needs to be done. Otherwise, students are always finding themselves behind, cramming on one subject to catch up, but at the same time getting themselves behind in other work.

There are other important reasons for blocking out a schedule for specific subjects. It enables you to assign less time to "easy" subjects than to "difficult" ones. It also *distributes,* rather than *masses,* study time. Psychologists have done an enormous amount of research on the "timing of learning," and this research underscores the need for distributing time. That is to say, in the long run you'll learn a lot more and remember it better if you spend eight different widely spaced hours studying something than if you spend eight consecutive hours studying it. Finally, there is a best time to study anything, depending on what it is. Certain subjects should be studied at certain times and not at others.

As a good general rule, a study period for a particular subject should come close to its class period. This rule doesn't mean that *all* the study time on a subject should be scheduled in this way but only that some of it should. The rule can be further subdivided into two parts: If the class time is mostly devoted to lecture rather than recitation, you should allocate a study period immediately *after* class. On the other hand, if class time is largely spent in recitation, you should schedule a period of review just *before* class. Some courses are pretty much all lecture or all recitation; others are a mixture. You should make up your schedule accordingly.

**Studying for lecture courses.** What do you do in a study period placed immediately *after* a lecture? You review the notes taken in class, first of all making sure that you understand them. Don't assume, since you were able to follow all the principal points made by the lecturer in class, that you have in fact assimilated them. It's easy to fall into this trap and to deceive yourself into thinking you have learned more than you actually have.

In most cases, unless the lecturer is unusually well organized and you are a top-notch note taker, you should revise or rewrite the notes. In doing that, eliminate any of the notes that now seem trivial or unimportant, and expand those you now can see are important. You can do this while the lecture is still fresh in mind,

## A SAMPLE SCHEDULE FOR A COLLEGE STUDENT

*This schedule is for a typical student carrying a moderately heavy load. Notice that the times set aside for study are labeled for specific subjects. Study time is about twenty-five hours per week; the student is also employed for ten hours a week.*

| Hour | Monday | Tuesday | Wednesday | Thursday | Friday | Saturday |
|------|--------|---------|-----------|----------|--------|----------|
| 7–8 | Dress, breakfast | Dress, breakfast | Dress, breakfast | Dress, breakfast | Dress, breakfast | |
| 8–9 | Econ. lect. | **Study econ.** | Econ. lect. | **Study psych.** | Econ. lect. | Dress, breakfast |
| 9–10 | **Study Ger.** | Eng.-lit. class | **Study Ger.** | Eng. class | **Study Ger.** | Org.-chem. lab. |
| 10–11 | Ger. class | **Study Ger.** | Ger. class | **Study Ger.** | Ger. class | Org.-chem. lab. |
| 11–12 | Psych. lect. | **Study Ger. or psych.** | Psych. lect. | **Study Ger. or psych.** | Psych. lect. | Org.-chem. lab. |
| 12–1 | Lunch | Lunch | Lunch | Lunch | Lunch | Lab. cont. or lunch |
| 1–2 | Org.-chem. lect. | **Study** or recreation | Org.-chem. lect. | **Study** or recreation | Org.-chem. lect. | Lunch or recreation |
| 2–3 | **Study org. chem.** | **Study psych.** | **Study org. chem.** | **Study psych.** | **Study org. chem.** | Recreation or **study** |
| 3–4 | **Study econ.** | ROTC or athletics | **Study econ.** | ROTC or athletics | **Study org. chem.** | Recreation or **study** |
| 4–5 | Employed | Employed | Employed | Employed | Employed | Recreation |
| 5–6 | Employed | Employed | Employed | Employed | Employed | Recreation |
| 6–7 | Dinner | Dinner | Dinner | Dinner | Dinner | Dinner |
| 7–8 | **Study Eng.** | **Study org. chem.** | **Study Eng.** | Study for subj. needing "catching up," library time | Recreation, make-up **study,** or library | Recreation |
| 8–9 | **Study Eng.** | **Study org. chem.** | **Study Eng.** | | | Recreation |
| 9–10 | | | | | | Recreation |

but you will find it a hopeless job if you let time pass and with it your memory. In revising your notes, you can also reorganize them so that they are more legible, better arranged, and in a more useful condition for subsequent reviews.

What do you do when a study period is put just *before* a class? If the class is a lecture, you can read the assignment that goes along with the lecture. Lecturers usually want students to read textbook assignments before lecture, especially in the larger introductory courses. Yet most students don't do this since no one checks up on them. Prereading, however, is a good rule of effective study, for the more you know about what the lecturer is saying, the more you learn in lecture and the better your notes generally are. You know better what is important and unimportant among the things the lecturer says, and the chances are you will be able to identify technical terms he doesn't explain clearly.

**Studying for recitation courses.** If a class is mostly recitation, as many language courses are, you can use the study period just before the class to get ready to recite. If the assignment is such that you can master it in an hour and be sure of it, this can be your principal study period. In many cases, though, this hour won't be enough, and you shouldn't take the chance that it will be enough. To be safe, you should go over the assignment at an earlier time and use the study period for review and for private recitation of what you have previously learned. In this way, you distribute study and bring yourself up to peak performance for the class. Consequently, not only will you do your best in class, but you will probably get more out of the class. Instead of depending on class to get you started in what you should have done for yourself, you now can count on the class to polish off the job you already have two-thirds done.

Incidentally, although students are taught all through school to be prepared, they only too often haven't learned the value of practicing the maxim. Not preparing *at the right time* keeps them hobbling through a course. In subjects such as language and mathematics, where knowledge and skills progress a step at a time, the consequences of poor preparation can be calamitous. Because a student hasn't prepared on time, he doesn't know what's going on in class and is hesitant about answering questions for fear he may reveal his ignorance. As the problems become more difficult, he is increasingly baffled both in outside study and in class because he hasn't kept up with what has gone before. The prepared student, on the other hand, takes each step in stride. Also he is no longer afraid of class or bored by it. Knowing what's going on and being the master of it, he finds learning interesting, even exciting. He can participate in classwork and take satisfaction in his progress. Thus he makes headway in the most difficult of all problems, the problem of having sufficient motivation and interest to study.

## HOW TO MAKE AND REVISE
## A SCHEDULE

We've explained why a study schedule is blocked out in hours and why certain subjects should be studied immediately before or after their class periods. Now we come to the question of how you should allot time to particular subjects. How do you plan and revise a study schedule? We say *plan* and *revise* because you can't just make up a schedule at the beginning of a term and never change it thereafter. You must revise it in the light of your experience with it. In any case, you must have a schedule, and *you* are the one who must make it.

**How much time?** The amount of time you allot to particular subjects depends, of course, on how much total study time you think you should budget. This is a highly individual matter. You must evaluate your own abilities and study habits. Most students, as we brought out in the last chapter, tend to overrate their own intelligence, speed of reading, ability to work, etc. It will therefore pay you to be critical of how much you can accomplish in an allotted time, especially if your ambition is high. Make sure, therefore, to budget enough time for your principal job in college, which is studying.

Don't overdo it, though. Leave realistic amounts of time for eating, sleeping, and leisure. Leisure is essential, not only because you must be rested and healthy to get the most out of college but because well-spent leisure is an essential part of a college education. In factories and offices—as well as in studies—when people attempt to put in very long hours, say, fifty-five to sixty hours a week, not only are they less happy and less efficient, they usually get less done than if they didn't work so many hours. That's why, in part at least, the grinding students who work thirty-five to fifty hours a week don't do as well as those who study less. There are exceptions, of course, but don't consider yourself one until you have proved it. Perhaps if you learn to work effectively in a shorter schedule of study, you will later be able to grind away harder and longer if need be. Starting out by trying to do too much, however, often leads one to give up altogether; and it is more important to have a moderate schedule that works than one that goes to pieces because it is impossibly ambitious.

**Allocating your time.** Now about the details of the schedule. Use the pages you will find for this purpose in the back of the book (they can be torn out by using a ruler). Start with the page labeled Provisional Working Schedule. As soon as you know when your classes and laboratories will be, fill these in. Next fill in the amount of time you spend eating and doing other daily routines. Now estimate how much time you will need for studying each of the various subjects you are taking. A good general rule for studying is that one to two hours of study time are required for each hour of lecture or recitation. You must modify this in the light of what you know about the probable difficulty of your courses *for you*.

You can make some estimate of difficulty by considering your own previous experience and training. If languages have always been relatively easy for you and sciences relatively hard, make allowance for that. If you feel your preparation for one course has been strong whereas that for another has been weak, adjust for that difference. This, of course, is obvious advice and most students take these points into account both in choosing their courses and in preparing for them. What they don't do, however, and what you must do, is think these and other questions through carefully at the outset and incorporate your estimates into a study schedule.

When you have made your best guesses about the work various courses are going to entail, you are now ready to fill in the details of your first provisional schedule. In deciding where to put periods for different subjects, keep in mind what was said about the study periods you put just before class and those you schedule just after class.

**An example.** To illustrate the process of making up a schedule, consider the sample schedule given on page 15. This student has allotted a total of twenty-three hours a week to study. In addition, he has provided for up to six additional hours to be used to catch up on something or to review for examinations. These "optional" hours, however, are not labeled, for they will be used as the occasion arises.

Of the five courses he's taking, he thinks organic chemistry will be his most difficult because it has a laboratory and requires laboratory reports. Then too, chemistry has never been easy for him. He therefore assigns six of his twenty-three hours to this subject. Three of them he puts immediately following the three weekly lectures. A fourth he puts on Friday to prepare for the laboratory on Saturday. The

## A DIARY OF TIME

*In order to discover how you are now using your time and to help you de-velop a realistic schedule for yourself, you ought to keep track of your time for at least a week. Make it a typical week of the regular schedule of classes and study. Either carry this book around with you or draw up some charts on cards that you may use for the purpose. Follow the example at the left of*

| EXAMPLE | | | MONDAY | | | TUESDAY | | | WEDNESDAY | | |
|---|---|---|---|---|---|---|---|---|---|---|---|
| Activity | Until | Time | Activity | Until | Time | Activity | Until | Time | Activity | Until | Time |
| Sleep | 7:30 | 8:00 | | | | | | | | | |
| Toilet | 7:55 | :25 | | | | | | | | | |
| Break. | 8:15 | :20 | | | | | | | | | |
| Study French | 9:00 | :45 | | | | | | | | | |
| Class | 10:00 | 1:00 | | | | | | | | | |
| Waste Time | 10:25 | :25 | | | | | | | | | |
| Study History | 11:00 | :35 | | | | | | | | | |
| Class | 12:00 | 1:00 | | | | | | | | | |
| Lunch | 12:25 | :25 | | | | | | | | | |
| Social | 1:00 | :35 | | | | | | | | | |
| Lab. | 4:00 | 3:00 | | | | | | | | | |
| Work | 6:00 | 2:00 | | | | | | | | | |
| Waste Time | 6:30 | :30 | | | | | | | | | |
| Dinner | 7:00 | :30 | | | | | | | | | |
| Reading | 7:20 | :20 | | | | | | | | | |
| Study Psychology | 8:15 | :55 | | | | | | | | | |
| Waste Time | 8:50 | :35 | | | | | | | | | |
| Study English | 10:00 | 1:10 | | | | | | | | | |
| Recreation | 11:15 | 1:15 | | | | | | | | | |
| Toilet | 11:30 | :15 | | | | | | | | | |
| Sleep | — | — | | | | | | | | | |

*the table as a guide in keeping the chart. Each time you start an activity, write it down in the column provided. Each time you finish that particular activity, note the time in the box beside the activity. Then by subtracting the time previously recorded from this time, figure out and write down in the right-hand box for the day the amount of time spent in this activity.*

| THURSDAY | | | FRIDAY | | | SATURDAY | | | SUNDAY | | |
|---|---|---|---|---|---|---|---|---|---|---|---|
| Activity | Until | Time | Activity | Until | Time | Activity | Until | Time | Activity | Until | Time |
| | | | | | | | | | | | |
| | | | | | | | | | | | |
| | | | | | | | | | | | |
| | | | | | | | | | | | |
| | | | | | | | | | | | |
| | | | | | | | | | | | |
| | | | | | | | | | | | |
| | | | | | | | | | | | |
| | | | | | | | | | | | |
| | | | | | | | | | | | |
| | | | | | | | | | | | |
| | | | | | | | | | | | |
| | | | | | | | | | | | |
| | | | | | | | | | | | |
| | | | | | | | | | | | |
| | | | | | | | | | | | |
| | | | | | | | | | | | |
| | | | | | | | | | | | |
| | | | | | | | | | | | |
| | | | | | | | | | | | |

## SUMMARY OF TIME DIARY

*Add up the times recorded for each activity in your time diary and enter the totals in the spaces below. Thus you'll be able to see just where your time is going and take steps to use it more profitably.*

| Activity | Monday | Tuesday | Wednesday | Thursday | Friday | Saturday | Sunday | Week's total |
|----------|--------|---------|-----------|----------|--------|----------|--------|--------------|
| Sleep | | | | | | | | |
| Meals | | | | | | | | |
| Classes | | | | | | | | |
| Study | | | | | | | | |
| Work | | | | | | | | |
| Social | | | | | | | | |
| Recreation | | | | | | | | |
| Campus activities | | | | | | | | |
| Waste time | | | | | | | | |
| Miscellaneous | | | | | | | | |
| Total | | | | | | | | |

last two he assigns to Tuesday night in order to have a longer stretch for writing up his lab report.

Of the remaining subjects, he thinks German may be most difficult partly because he hasn't been tops in languages, partly because the German course has a reputation for being one of the more difficult courses, and partly because he knows there is a lot of memorizing and translating to do. He therefore assigns five hours to this and also provides for a couple more that may be spent on it (or on psychology) if necessary. Of the five regularly scheduled hours, he puts three just before the three classes each week because German is primarily a recitation class in which he may be called upon to translate.

In planning for his other three subjects, he thinks economics will probably be the easiest.

He comes from a business family, did well in this sort of thing in high school, and has read widely in business magazines. Furthermore, campus grapevine has it that the text is rather easy reading and that the instructor puts the greatest emphasis on lectures. He therefore assigns three hours a week, about the minimum, to economics and puts two of these hours as close after lecture as he can. He can't do any better than that if he is to give priority to organic chemistry and German, which are his toughest subjects.

So far, he hasn't given too much attention in his planning to English literature because he can study that almost any time. The big job in this course will be to read rapidly a great number of pages of outside reading. This material doesn't have to be learned in detail like a textbook, nor will it be difficult to comprehend. He'll just have to read it and know the gist of it so that he'll be prepared for the discussion in class. He therefore sets aside a couple of hours on two evenings each week to get this reading done.

That leaves psychology. He hasn't had any courses before in psychology, for this frequently isn't taught in high school. It shouldn't be too hard, and reports are that it isn't. Moreover, according to the outline of the course he received on the first day of class, his main job is to study the textbook. The lectures, according to the teacher, will be mainly to explain and illustrate the book. So he decides to assign it, like economics, the minimum of three hours a week and to schedule them in the odd spaces he still has left in his morning and afternoon schedule. He is uncertain, though, whether this will be enough, just as he did not know whether five hours a week would be enough for German. So he sets aside two hours that can be used for either German or psychology, depending on how things go in these courses.

Of course, this is a first approximation of the total amount of time he'll need for studying and of the amount assigned to each course. To play safe, he had better have, say, six additional hours available in case any of his estimates have proved too low. He'll undoubtedly need them when hour exams come around, and perhaps at other times. Otherwise, he can use them the way he pleases. These extra hours are chosen and put down in his schedule as either recreation or study.

Totaling up his accounts, he can expect to be in class or laboratory about seventeen hours a week, studying from twenty-three to twenty-nine hours a week, and working ten hours a week at a part-time job. This is quite a bit; yet he has a good deal of time left over. He doesn't have to burn the midnight oil and, in fact, can plan on knocking off about ten o'clock each night for a snack, bull session, or other recreation. He has leisurely meal hours for restful breaks in his work; there is time for some exercise; and beginning with Saturday afternoon, his whole week end is free. Some of the time, too, he can expect to take one or two

extra evenings off a week. Though this schedule calls for more study than most students actually do, it is still one of great leisure compared with the schedule of a doctor, lawyer, or businessman or the one the student himself is likely to have when he is well launched on his career.

**Revising the schedule.** Your first schedule for the semester should not be your last. The chances are that you will have planned too much or too little time for various activities. You may have been too unrealistic about how much total time you spend in studying. If so, make a compromise. Use the schedule as a kind of goal to work toward, particularly if you are not doing as well as you should. But, above all, be realistic. Your schedule will do you no good at all if it is so unrealistic that you can't follow it at all in practice. Make a workable schedule, and perhaps after you begin to acquire regular habits of work, you can begin to revise your schedule to make it more like your original goals.

Once you have regular habits of study, you don't need to rely on your schedule as an incentive. You can use it just as a convenient plan for your week's activities.

We have provided four schedule sheets for you to use in making revisions in your schedule. Perhaps you will need more. If so, you can make up some additional ones for yourself. You probably ought not to change your schedule more than once every two weeks, and ordinarily not oftener than every three or four weeks, for you ought to know how one schedule has worked for a week or two before you revise it. And you probably shouldn't make drastic, sweeping revisions all at once. Any changes should be made by reassigning only a few hours at a time. Otherwise, you'll be so confused you won't have a schedule. When you have a schedule that seems to work well, with or without a few minor changes, make out the Final Working Schedule you'll find in the back of the book.

We should mention incidentally that you ought to keep your schedule where you can refer to it easily. In fact, you ought to have it where you can't miss seeing it several times a day and thus have it as a reminder of what you should be doing. One good place is the front of your notebook, which should be your constant companion. Another, if you do most of your studying in your room, is on the wall above your desk or in a similarly visible place.

## HOW TO USE YOUR TIME

Many students set up a schedule and don't find it to be of much help because they can't make it work. They can't seem to do what the schedule calls for. Though they start off with good intentions, they can't manage to study when they're supposed to.

**Are you a dribbler?**    Here's what happened, for example, to one student whose schedule was to read English literature from seven until ten o'clock. Determined to do his reading on schedule, he sat down at his desk promptly at seven. First, he discovered that his pencil needed sharpening before he could make any notes. He ran across the hall to the room of a friend who had a sharpener. There he found an interesting discussion going on about the merits of Fords versus Chevrolets. Becoming absorbed in this, it was some time before he remembered that he was supposed to be studying English. Starting back to his room, he recalled that there was a good radio program on. With the aid of a little wishful thinking, he convinced himself that it was just as easy to read English with the radio on as off. Next, with his attention divided between the radio and the book, he found himself gazing absently at a picture on his desk that conjured up fond memories of the last week end. And so it went. Ten o'clock came, time to go out for a hamburger—and still no work done.

This dribbling away of time is the major stumbling block to effective study. Countless surveys of students have shown this to be true; and if you've been in college long, you've no doubt seen it for yourself. If this is your problem, and it probably is, try to solve it slowly and carefully. It can be solved, but it takes practice and determination.

Start by making your study periods short and planning on brief periods of rest or relaxation in between. Instead of trying to study three hours at one crack and accomplishing nothing, settle for one hour at a time. It is much more important to work effectively for short periods than to schedule long ones and fritter them away in aimless procrastination. If you set for yourself a modest target, it will be easier to hit. You won't find the prospects so forbidding, and you'll be more likely to do what you set out to do. Then you'll at least have accomplished something. If necessary, cut yourself down to very short periods, say, of twenty minutes, and take ten minutes off deliberately; then go back to work for another twenty. Indeed, use any device you can to make yourself work for some definite period of time. The essential thing is to actually work when you are supposed to.

Once you have gotten into the swing of an easy schedule of work and rest, you can gradually change it. The important thing is to make yourself study with all the concentration you can muster while you are studying. Managing that and experiencing the satisfaction that comes from concentrated work, you can then lengthen the periods. Even so, they probably shouldn't be too long. Even those who are proficient at studying and creative efforts and who are able to keep at their work more or less continuously for long hours usually find that they need short breaks every hour or so to keep themselves alert and rested and thus able to make the most of their working periods.

**Where to study.**    Students would certainly conquer their problems of getting down to work more easily if others would cooperate with them. Unfortunately, most other people in your dormitory, your fraternity or sorority house, or your own home work on a different schedule and are no more disciplined in getting down to work than you are. They pop into your room and start a discussion, or they have something interesting going on within earshot, and the temptation proves too great. In the war against frittered time, our roommates, friends, and relatives are our worst enemies.

That's why it is usually better to find some place to work where other people can't bother you. In a college, the best place is probably the library, near the back and facing a wall rather than near the door. Libraries are set up for people to study in and they have rules against talking and other distractions. They even protect the student against himself, for they have no radios to turn on and no sweetheart's picture to look at, and they make one somewhat more embarrassed to be seen daydreaming. It's no surprise, then, that surveys show that students who habitually study in the library make better grades than other students.

Some students, though, claim they feel uncomfortable in the library. Perhaps that is because they are not really motivated to study or are afraid they'll miss out on a good time at the dormitory or fraternity house. It may be due partly to the fact that studying in strange surroundings is more difficult than in familiar ones. And libraries are indeed strange places to many students. The remedy, of course, is to get acquainted with the library so that it seems like a normal place to be. If then you make up your mind to study in the library and go there only when you really intend to study, you should find it a good place to get some work done.

Although libraries, on the whole, are good places to study, some people can and do study effectively in other places—in their rooms, on park benches, on busses and trains. You probably can too after you have really learned to study. If you are still learning the art, though, it's safer to pick a library or similar place and then graduate later to working under more distracting circumstances.

More and more dormitories, fraternities, and student centers are setting up special places for study which are quiet and well designed for studying. If you have some special prejudice against the library as a place to study, one of these places is a satisfactory substitute.

**Physical conditions.**   Good physical conditions of study can help you considerably in your efforts to work effectively on a schedule and to accomplish what you want to. The best place to study is at a table or desk, not on a bed. Bed is a little too relaxing and doesn't go along

Study is best done at an uncluttered desk free of distractions.

naturally with the work that studying is. Sitting up straight and keeping muscles reasonably tense may require more effort, but it also keeps one alert and in the mood for work.

A clean desk is a better place to work than a desk cluttered with mementos and pictures. Besides providing the space in which to spread out one's work, it gets rid of distracting influences that all too easily set one to daydreaming and frittering away time. Put the pictures, radio, and trophies some place else in the room so you won't see them when you study. For the same reason, a desk that faces the wall offers a little better protection against distraction than one that faces a window or door. You just won't see people passing by; and when they see you, they'll know you're working and will be less likely to interrupt you.

Good lighting that floods the entire working area is also an important condition for effective study. If you have to hunch and squint to see your work, you tire easily and give up more quickly. Hence lighting that is adequate, comfortable, and pleasant will keep motivation up longer and make studying a more inviting task.

## CORRECTING POOR STUDY CONDITIONS

*Consider thoughtfully each of the questions below, and write down specific answers to each one. Then figure out what you can do about each of the things that is wrong with your study conditions. Make notes on these and then set about correcting the difficulties.*

| Things that are wrong | What to do to correct them |
|---|---|
| What can you see on your desk and through your window or door to distract you? | |
| What music, talking, or other noises are disturbing your study? | |
| What is wrong with your position and posture when you study? | |
| Are you sure your lighting is adequate? What's wrong with it? | |
| Is your work space large enough and arranged well? | |
| What materials for effective study don't you have at hand? | |
| What times of day is it most difficult for you to study? Why? | |
| What worries or special interests divert you from studying? | |

LET'S ASSUME that you have worked out a schedule, found a good place to study, and want to study. You're at a library table or desk with all your materials in front of you, and you know what you want to study for the next hour. Now the problem is to make the best possible use of the hour. In the time allotted, you want to learn as much as you can, you want to learn the important things and bypass the trivial, and you want to remember what you study. Let's find out what the best way to go about it is.

Every student, of course, has his own approach and his own techniques. Two different students, each outstanding, will often go about studying the same material in somewhat different ways. That is to be expected, for different techniques are suited to different people. There are, nevertheless, general rules for effective study. People who are good at studying make some use of these rules, in one way or another, whether or not they realize it. They will differ mainly in their individual styles and in the degree to which they put reliance on different rules.

What are these rules? One way of phrasing them simply has been worked out at Ohio State University in an elaborate program for analyzing and treating students' academic problems. In this program, the essential rules are condensed into the following formula: *Survey Q 3R*. Say this over to yourself a few times in order to commit it to memory because it is a good slogan for carrying out a course of effective study.

# THREE

# THE STRATEGY OF

# STUDY

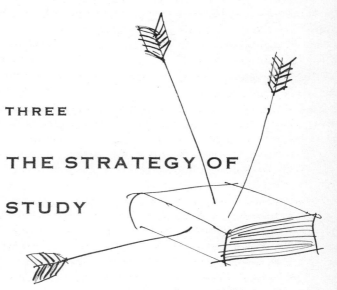

This phrase is a way of summarizing five specific steps in effective study:

*Survey*
*Question*
*Read*
*Recite*
*Review*

The *Survey Q 3R* program has been soundly tested. It has been proved not only to describe what good students do but to be a safe guide for improving enormously the work that all students, good and poor, can do. This chapter will consider in detail each of its five steps.

## SURVEY

The first of the five steps is survey. It tells you that you should get the best possible over-all

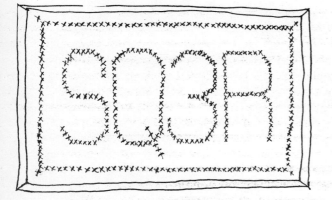

To conclude your survey of the book as a whole, there are two further things to do. One is to leaf through it, and the other is to read the summaries of the chapters (if there are summaries). In two or three hours you can turn every page of a substantial textbook, glancing at the headings and reading occasional sentences under them. And it is well worth the trouble since it gives you a feel for the book and an understanding of its over-all organization. If your book has summaries, read them all as part of your initial survey of the book. The bird's-eye view you obtain in this way is of incalculable value.

picture of what you are going to study before you study it in any detail. Such a perspective is important in study for the same reason that people consult maps before they drive unfamiliar roads, that expert golf players want to walk around a new course before they actually play it, or that a road builder makes a detailed survey of the terrain before he starts construction of a road. In each case, the person wants to know what he is going to run into before he starts; he needs to know the general picture before he can make intelligent decisions about the details.

**Surveying a chapter.**    Now let's turn from the initial survey to what you do when you sit down to read an assigned chapter. You should survey the chapter, but more carefully than you've done for the book, and this time with an eye especially on the headings.

When most authors write textbooks, they go to some pains to organize their words under various headings. In fact, the time they spend planning their headings, putting them in the right places, and phrasing them so that they will tell as much as possible is often a good chunk of the time they spend in writing. They do this partly so the student can know what to expect as he reads—in other words, survey—and partly to make later reviewing much easier. In most textbooks you will find scarcely a page without a heading on it.

**Surveying a book.**    Surveying a book must proceed in steps, from big ones to little ones. When you first pick up a book, a good thing to do is to survey the whole book. Start the survey by reading the preface, for in it the author quickly gives you an idea of why he wrote the book and what he will attempt to do in it. By reading what the author has to say, you can find out what kind of book it is and whom it is for and not for. It may even tell you what preparation and knowledge is required for reading the book. In any case, the preface usually gives some clear picture of what is to come.

Next in any book comes the table of contents. Look at it, go through it slowly and thoughtfully, find out from it as much as you can about what the book contains. Moreover, you should do this repeatedly as you progress through the course. The farther you read in the book the more meaningful the table of contents becomes.

Yet many students ignore the headings and try to read textbooks the way they would novels. When they do that, they ignore much of the author's careful work, and more important, they throw away the most significant and useful clues to the contents of the book.

One important precept, then, is *use the headings.* They give you the author's organization, they tell you how the material is put together, and they make it clear how topics go together and follow each other. Most important, they make it clear what the main subject of each section is going to be. When you finish reading a section, you should have located certain points that bear on the heading. Anything else in the section will be secondary or relatively unimportant.

You should also pay attention to the *order of headings*. Most textbooks use two or three orders. This one, for example, has two: main headings on separate lines and run-in side headings. There are two or more side headings under each main heading, and this arrangement tells you what topics are subordinate to the main topics. In many textbooks, there is still another (lower) order of heading, indicated by a different kind of type, usually italic. These indicate sub-subheadings under the subheadings, which in turn come under the main headings. Note the kinds of heading used, for they are the key to the structure of the subject you are studying.

We have told you in detail about headings because you must use them at several stages in the study process. You use them in making a general, initial survey of the book, and then you go over them again as part of your detailed survey of an assigned chapter. The first thing to do, in picking up a textbook to read a chapter, is to run through the headings in the chapter. In this way, you learn generally what the chapter is about and know what to expect. It is also a good idea to skim some of the sentences here and there in the chapter and to look at some of the pictures and charts.

In addition, if there is a summary, read this as part of your chapter survey. It will give you the most important points of the chapter before details begin to clutter up the picture.

This concludes what we have to say about the survey step in *Survey Q 3R* methods. We have dwelt on it and emphasized it for two reasons: First of all, we know from experience and systematic research that most students do not do enough surveying. They have acquired habits of plunging into the woods without first getting a map of the footpaths in it. Secondly, we know that survey methods pay great dividends. In several programs in which thousands of students have been taught to use survey methods, the students have made remarkable gains, by actual measurement, in their ability to comprehend and learn new material.

## QUESTION

The *Q* in *Survey Q 3R* means question, and it emphasizes the importance of asking questions for learning. Most things worth remembering in textbooks or in life, more generally, are answers to some sort of question. Moreover, people seem to remember what they learn in answer to a question better than things just read or memorized.

Questions help learning because they make us think about what it is we want to know about what we are reading or studying. They give a purpose to our learning. A person with a question is a person with a purpose. The answers to our own questions make an impression on us because they make what we are studying more meaningful to us, and we always remember something better when it means something very specific to us.

**Your questions.** If you make use of the question technique in reading this book, you should already have a number of them about this section: Why does the author have a heading about questions? What do questions have to do with studying? What good are questions? How can I use them in studying? Whose questions? Where do they come from? How do I know when they are answered? These are some of the questions you might have asked by now. Some of them are already partly answered, and if you keep them in mind, you will find that the rest will be answered shortly.

Who asks the questions? The best source is yourself. You are the one who is trying to learn and who will be helped by asking them. Every time you see a heading, questions should come rushing to mind. At the very least, you should ask what the word or phrase means. If you know its dictionary definition, you should be curious about its meaning in the present context.

Now you might be asking yourself a new question, "I know I'm supposed to be asking questions, but I'm not used to doing that. How do I acquire the skill?" The answer to this one, like answers to so many such questions, is "It takes practice." Knowing that questions are aids to study, you should begin working at the technique in everything you study. At first, to emphasize the method, you might write down questions when you survey a chapter, as you are running through the headings and skimming the topic sentences of paragraphs. This is laborious and too time-consuming to be done as a regular thing, but it might get you off the

## THE USE OF QUESTIONS IN STUDYING

*Here is a sample paragraph from a textbook (Arden N. Frandsen,* How Children Learn, *McGraw-Hill, New York, 1957, p. 414). The kinds of question you would want to ask about this material are written in.*

*What is homogeneous grouping?*

*What IQ ranges?*

*what should be done with the homogeneous groups?*

2. *Homogeneous Grouping.* A plan for adjusting to the individual differences in mental ability of pupils of the same age, applicable in large schools, is to classify children in each grade into sections according to IQs. If the school population is large enough, three sections of equal size can be arranged in each grade by classifying in the highest section pupils whose IQs are 108 and higher, in the middle section children with IQs from 93 through 107, and in the lowest section children whose IQs are 60 through 92. For these three sections of each grade, now more homogeneous with respect to IQ, there should be three differentiated curricula. The middle group should progress through school with the usual curriculum. For the highest group, the curriculum should be enriched. And for the lowest group, the curriculum should consist of minimum essentials and should aim at more limited academic goals.

*To what kind of schools should homogeneous grouping apply?*

*Here is another paragraph from the same source (pp. 414, 415). Try writing your own questions. See how they compare with the questions listed on page 30.*

Homogeneous grouping was invented and became popular early in the history of intelligence testing in schools. Uniform assignments, general recitations, and other activities conducted with the class as a whole are considered easier to manage when pupils are grouped homogeneously. In general, the research on ability grouping has revealed "slightly superior achievement and better personal adjustment" for homogeneous than for heterogeneous groups [77]. Barthelmess and Boyer [5] found for equated groups of fourth grade pupils an achievement gain of 12.8 months for homogeneous classes during a school year, while heterogeneous classes gained 10.4 months. Sorenson, however, considers the evaluative evidence on ability grouping "far from adequate" [77, p. 237]. And in at least one comparative study [23], the gain in reading achievement for fifth and sixth grade pupils was slightly greater for the group of wider IQ range than for the narrower-range group.

ground. When you have cultivated the questioning frame of mind, you may simply think your questions out to yourself as you survey and later as you read the chapter. Eventually, the art of asking questions becomes so ingrained that you don't have to stop to formulate them. They flood in as you read along; as they get answered, the answers raise new questions without your consciously trying to ask them.

**The author's questions.** You can secure some help in acquiring questioning skills from textbooks and workbooks. Authors occasionally ask questions as part of their teaching technique and in some cases start off each chapter with a list of questions to be answered in the body of the chapter. Be alert to them and use them. In some textbooks, authors have listed questions at the end of each chapter. Such questions are usually the most neglected part of a textbook, for students do not realize their value in studying. You should read them as part of your survey of a chapter, then again after you have finished reading it. Used in this way, the questions help you study the chapter, providing a means of testing yourself. If you test yourself before the instructor does, you do much better when faced with a formal examination.

Now stop for a second. In starting to read this section, did you pause to ask questions? What are author's questions? Are they in the book? Where? Where are the answers?

Nowadays many textbooks are accompanied by student workbooks which the student can obtain and use separately. Very frequently the workbook contains several kinds of questions, some to be used in studying and in reviewing and others that are samples of the kind of examination you can expect to take. When such questions are available, make the fullest possible use of them. Faster learning, more fun studying, and better grades are practically guaranteed!

## READ

The next part of *Survey Q 3R* is to read. This is the part too many students put first, for they mistakenly think that studying is mostly a mat-ter of running their eyes over the textbook. The book is, of course, to be read, but this is neither the first, last, nor even necessarily the most important part of studying. It's only the trip through the woods made after the terrain has been surveyed and the path mapped out by questions. It enables one to mark the big trees and the points of interest so that they can easily be found later when the trip is made more hurriedly (review) or be pointed out to someone else (recitation and examination).

Despite the fact that students spend relatively too much time trying to read, many don't know how to do it as well as they ought to. They regularly get themselves lost while reading; they waste a lot of time tramping around in the brush of trivia; they never see the large landmarks of concepts and conclusions. Few students ever learn craftsmanlike reading.

We will look at this point a little later on when we devote a whole chapter to the art of reading. It takes a chapter, in fact, to explain how to read, for there are a lot of things to do when you read. If we tried to discuss them here, we would be taken far off our main path. So all we will do now is give you a few pointers that belong in the picture of the five steps in the *Survey Q 3R* method.

**Read actively.** When you read for studying, do not read passively as you would an adventure novel. Such novels are for entertainment, and they are written without any concern for whether you remember the details. Most textbooks, on the other hand, have structures that must be explored. You can't just walk through them; you must be alert to your surroundings every step of the way. To avoid passive reading, read to answer the questions you have asked yourself or the questions the instructor or author has asked. As you go along, keep challenging yourself to make sure that you understand what you read.

Every once in a while, remind yourself of your task: to understand and remember what you read. If you do, you will no longer voice the familiar complaint "I forget what I read as soon as I am through."

Some of the really important novels, incidentally, deserve the same kind of reading that textbooks do, even though some of the specific recommendations for avoiding passive reading that you will find in this section will not apply to reading novels or stories.

**Note important terms.**  Notice especially any words or phrases that are italicized. Authors use these, like headings, to emphasize important terms, concepts, and principles. They are a warning to stop and take heed—that here is something more important than the rest the author is saying. Say these terms to yourself a few times. Make sure you know how to spell them (instructors get a little impatient with students who can't spell even the important words). Then make sure you note and understand what is said about them.

**Read everything.**  When you read, too, read *everything*. That means tables, graphs, and other illustrations as well as the main text. They are there for a purpose, not just to make the page attractive or to fill up space. Textbook writers never have enough space to cover all they want to say, and when they use their precious space for tables and illustrations, they think these will teach better than words. They actually will if you use them. Sometimes a mere glance at an illustration will tell vividly what a whole page of the book is about. In other cases, illustrations convey information that cannot be expressed easily in words, no matter how many of them were used. Remember the old adage "A picture is worth a thousand words"? Sometimes this is very true, and the same is true of tables. Although tables are not so easy to grasp as pictures, they tell a story if you only take the

trouble to read and compare carefully the different columns in the table.

## RECITE

Recitation is an old, well-established way of learning and of examining. Before books were invented and in areas of the world where books are still scarce, it is the heart of learning. The teacher says something to his pupils and then asks them questions about what they have learned. They recite their answers. Oral recitation is a particularly handy teaching device when something must be learned by rote. We've probably all done it at one time or another in the lower grades of public school in memorizing the multiplication table, in learning the catechism of a church, or even in learning foreign languages in college.

**Value of recitation.**  What most students don't realize, however, is that recitation is also an effective device for learning while reading a book. So long as you just read a book, you have the comfort of thinking that you understand and can remember what you read. It is an unpleasant fact, as you no doubt have discovered at one time or another, that you do not necessarily remember all you feel you easily understand and remember. And the only way you can really find out what you remember is to recite to yourself. Because recitation can reveal your ignorance to yourself, it is one of several reasons why recitation is such an effective study method.

To make certain that you understand and remember, you should stop periodically and try to recall to yourself what you have read. This is recitation. At this point, for example,

## YOUR QUESTIONS

*The following are the sorts of questions you can ask in studying the passage on page 28.*

1. When was homogeneous grouping first employed?
2. What seem to be its advantages?
3. What has been the general result of research on

homogeneous grouping?
4. Is there adequate evidence for the general superiority of homogeneous grouping?

you might ask yourself what you have read so far in this chapter. Try to recall the main headings and the principal ideas under each heading. Can you give a synopsis of your reading without looking at the pages? Try to do it; then check yourself. See whether you have covered everything. If not, note your omissions and errors. Then a little later, recite again.

The general rule, then, is as follows: As you read, stop at intervals to recite the substance of each major section of a chapter. When you review for examinations, again make recitation a substantial part of your study procedure.

Don't think, though, that this is merely a good but rather incidental rule. Recitation can make all the difference in the world in how much you remember. If you read a prose passage such as this straight through, the chances are that you will remember *when you finish* no more than 50 per cent of the points made in it. The forgetting process has been going on even while you were reading. It continues, of course, to do its destructive work, and a day later you remember no more than 25 or 30 per cent. After that, memory fades more slowly, for there is less to lose, but at the end of two weeks you will probably remember no more than 10 per cent.

This is the course of forgetting when you don't recite. The actual percentage retained depends on how much you read, what kind of material it was, and on individual differences in memory ability. The percentages given above, however, were the ones actually obtained in a study of several thousand high-school students who were given tests to measure how much they remembered at different times after reading passages of prose. Some of the groups in this study, however, were "recitation groups." They recited what they could remember from their reading, two groups immediately after reading (one of these recited twice) and other groups at later times. When they were tested three weeks later, the group with two recitations immediately after studying remembered 80 per cent of what it knew when it finished reading, but a group with no intervening recitation knew only a sixth as much. Another way of

stating these results: The no-recitation group forgot more in one day than the recitation group did in sixty-three days! This difference was produced by a relatively brief recitation immediately after reading.

**How much recitation.**   How much time should you spend on recitation? This depends on what it is you are studying. If what you are learning is disconnected and not too meaningful, recitation should run as high as 90 or 95 per cent of your study time. If, for example, you have to learn a number of rules, items, names, laws, or formulas, then recitation will be your principal form of study. On the other hand, for well-organized, storylike material, such as one may find in history or philosophy, less recitation is needed. In this case, recitation might be no more than 20 or 30 per cent of the study

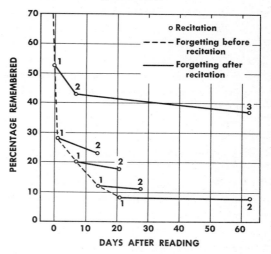

**VALUE OF RECITATION**

*(y-axis: PERCENTAGE REMEMBERED; x-axis: DAYS AFTER READING)*

o Recitation
– – – Forgetting before recitation
—— Forgetting after recitation

Each solid line represents the forgetting of a group of high-school students. All groups read the same material, but each group had different opportunities to recite what it had learned. The numbers indicate the number of recitations each group had. The top solid line, for example, represents a group that had three recitations, one immediately after learning, a second seven days later, and a third one sixty-three days later. (*Redrawn from H. F. Spitzer, "Studies in Retention," Journal of Educational Psychology, 30:641–656, 1939.*)

time. For textbooks in psychology, economics, political science, and the like, something of the order of 50 per cent is a good estimate, though even in these subjects books can vary quite a bit in "meaningfulness."

This you can be sure of: The time spent in recitation pays off. In one study, for example, students who spent up to 80 per cent of their time on recitation did better than people who spent the same time reading without reciting. You can also be sure that time spent in recitation actually saves time. The amount you remember by reciting is so great that you don't have to spend nearly so much time later in rereading the material and in reviewing it for an examination.

**When to recite.**    When should you recite? To wait until you have finished a chapter is usually to wait too long. You are already too hazy about the chapter's contents. Forgetting has taken its toll. On the other hand, stopping to recite after every paragraph or two may break up the material into too many disconnected pieces. For most prose like this, the section set off by a heading is probably the best unit. Each time you see a new heading come up, stop and recite the material in the section you have just finished. Do this for each side heading; then double up when you come to a main heading.

Besides improving your memory and saving time, recitation has other benefits: One is that it serves to keep your attention on your task. While you are merely reading, you may attend with only "half a mind" and even find your eyes moving along without learning anything. On the other hand, you certainly can't daydream while you are trying to recall something. In the second place, recitation lets you correct mistakes. It shows you where you missed something or where you misunderstood it. If you make notes of these mistakes when you recite, you know what points give your memory or understanding the most trouble. You can then concentrate on these when you later reread or review the material.

## REVIEW

The fifth and final precept of *Survey Q 3R* is review. We don't need to emphasize this because most students do review, especially before an examination. Many of them even review

## THE INTERPRETATION OF GRAPHS

*The preceding graph is fairly complicated as graphs go, and for that reason makes a good exercise in the study and interpretation of graphs. Here are some questions you might ask and answer in studying the graph. Write down your answers.*

1. How much was retained after one reading of the material?

2. What does the dotted line represent?

3. When does recitation do the most good? When does it do practically no good?

4. What is the general shape of a curve of forgetting? How does recitation change it?

things they haven't read before. There are a few comments worth making, however, about what review is and when it should be done.

**Survey.** Review isn't, of course, really very different from the other things that have gone before. In fact, it is all of them put together. A review is, first of all, a survey. Only it is a survey of what one is supposed to have done, rather than what he is going to do! It is done in much the same way as the original survey except that it can be combined with other steps in *Survey Q 3R*. When you now skim over the headings of the book, you can ask yourself what they mean and what they have under them. Under each of the headings, you can recite the points that you have previously read and that you hope you remember.

**Rereading.** You should reread enough to check yourself and see either that you haven't left anything out or that your memory is refreshed. The same is true when you now review the summaries. Instead of reading them as you did originally, you now see if you can recite them, and then you check yourself by rereading to see how well you know what is in the summaries. In reviewing, you will also go over notes you have taken on the book and on classroom work. (We haven't said anything yet about taking notes because we have reserved that for Chapter Five.)

**Timing of reviews.** If you have followed well the first four precepts under *Survey Q 3R,* you won't have much trouble knowing what to do when you review. You may not know, however, just when you should review and how often you should review. At least, most students don't. They review at the wrong times, and they don't review enough. They usually wait until they are face to face with an examination before they do their reviewing. That's a good time for a final review, but not for the first review.

The first time to review is immediately after you have studied something. For example, after you have read a chapter, reciting between each of its sections, you should immediately go back

and review it. This means trying to recite the important points of the whole chapter and rereading as necessary to check yourself. It also means reading over and then reciting the notes you have made on it (see Chapter Five). This first review may be fairly brief, for there has been little time for forgetting; and as we have implied, it should be mainly one of recitation.

It will pay you, though, to have one or two reviews between this first review and the final review for an examination. These intervening reviews usually should emphasize rereading more than recitation. They are to remind you of some of the fine points or examples that go along with the main points you have in your notes and, presumably, in your head.

The final review, the one just before an examination, should, like the first review, emphasize recitation. It should be more intensive —and usually is. In this, you go over all you are responsible for on the examination, paying special attention to the earlier material, which has had more of a chance to fade away. But plan your time so that you review *all* the material, and don't run out of time when you are about half through. It should go without saying, too, though many students need to be reminded of it, that reviewing should not be crammed into the last few hours before an examination. This practice makes the final task too hard. And it never gives you at the time of the examination the mastery you could have with a few well-spaced reviews.

The five steps in *Survey Q 3R* have been tried with thousands of college students in how-to-study programs. Students who have learned them and applied them have improved their grades—sometimes enormously— and have found satisfaction in study that they never knew before. You can too, even if you are already a fairly good student!

There are different ways of balancing the *Survey Q 3R* methods for your particular courses. French takes a different approach than physics, and English a different combination than psychology. In later chapters we'll come to some of the problems of studying such different subjects.

## SUMMARIZING A CHAPTER

*To practice what we have been teaching, the time to recite what you have read in this chapter is now. In the space that follows, write a synopsis of the chapter. Make it in outline form with plenty of space between the lines. When you have written down all you can recall, run back through the chapter and see what you have left out or not gotten quite right. Then make the appropriate additions and corrections in your synopsis.*

NEARLY EVERY STUDENT of college age has been reading for at least ten or eleven years and for two or three hours a day. In college he'll have to read more than that.

Yet the simple fact is that most college students don't know how to read well. Most are too slow, take much too much time, and don't learn or understand nearly as much as they could or should.

Something can be done about this, and it's a big part of learning how to study. A lot of advice we've already given you assumes that you can or will learn how to read better, but we have said little about it thus far because we intended to tell you about reading all in one place—here. As you'll see, you can increase your reading speed by a large margin, probably doubling it, and you can know a lot more when you're through.

## READING WITH A PURPOSE

The typical student who has an assignment to do says to himself, "I've got to read this chapter." Then he sits down and reads it—just reads it. He reads everything about the same way, English, history, chemistry, and so forth. He plods through the sentences like a man trudging to work, and when he's through, he says, "I've read it."

That's not the way to do it at all. There are many different ways to read, different things to look for and learn, and different speeds to read at. Which way one reads depends on his purpose. In fact, in studying college assignments, you should "read" the same material

## FOUR

# READING

# BETTER AND FASTER

two, three, or four times, each time with a different purpose. You must know before you start what your purpose is, and read accordingly.

**Getting the main idea.** One purpose in reading is merely to get the main idea. All you want to end up with is one sentence that expresses the nub of the passage. This is one of the things, but only one, that you want to do when you study. It's the thing you're after in the very first stage of studying, which is to survey. In doing this, you scan headings and skim sentences to give you the main topics and ideas of the chapter. It's also what you're after when you settle down to reading the assignment more carefully. Even though you will want more than the ideas, it's essential to pick them out; otherwise, nothing else will be meaningful or remembered well.

How do you find main ideas? This depends

on what you want the main idea of—chapter, section, subsection, or paragraph. Let's start with the paragraph, for this is the smallest unit. The usual definition of a paragraph, in fact, is that it contains one, and only one, idea. Most writers of textbooks know it, and they've usually put one idea in each of their paragraphs. Your job is to find it.

You may remember an old precept about writing: that you begin a paragraph with a topic sentence, then explain it, illustrate it, support it with additional sentences, and finally wind up with a summary sentence. To have the topic sentence, the idea sentence, come first in a paragraph is not, however, always practicable or desirable. Sometimes there has to be a transition or introductory sentence between the idea of the last paragraph and the idea of the present one. Such a sentence shows the student how one idea is connected with another one, but it shouldn't be mistaken for the main idea. Sometimes the author holds back his main idea for artistic reasons.

In looking for the main idea, don't look always for a whole sentence, for the idea is likely to be only a part of a sentence. It may be the principal clause or phrase in a sentence, and you usually can boil it down in your own mind to a couple of words. To see what we mean, pick up one of your textbooks and find some sentences with main ideas. Now try throwing away some of the adjectives and adverbs that don't materially change the meaning and keep only the subject, verb, and predicate. If you remember these key words, you can always supply the supporting words yourself.

When you do this, though, don't be too free and easy. Sometimes qualifiers are essential to the meaning. If we say, for example, "The fast reader is usually the fast learner," you can't omit the "usually." We don't mean that fast readers are always fast learners or that fast reading is synonymous with fast learning. We mean that, typically, often, most of the time, or on the average, fast readers manage to learn faster. On the other hand, if we say, "The person who reads rapidly, scanning each line in three or four glances and not stopping to day-

dream, is typically the person who learns a great deal in a short period of time," you can eliminate most of these words, translate them, and come up with "The fast reader is usually the fast learner" as your main idea.

We should point out in passing that you may encounter paragraphs in which the main idea is not expressed in a single sentence or even made explicit at all. That won't happen often in textbooks, but it will in descriptive writing, literature, and fiction. A story writer may, for example, spend a paragraph describing in minute detail the clothes one of his characters is wearing. He wants to tell you the kind of person the character is without flatly saying it, and so he leaves it to you to extract the character's personality from a vivid description. In that case, you can't find any sentences or group of words expressing the main idea; you simply have to devise your own summary of the paragraph. Keep this in mind when you're studying literature and, more generally, any descriptive writing. Sometimes a skillful writer of fiction can use this technique of spreading the essential idea over a whole paragraph to suggest many different things at once about a character or event in the story.

Make a habit of finding the main idea in every paragraph you read. When you think you've found it, check your conclusion by holding the idea in mind as you read on through the paragraph and compare it especially with the summary sentence. If you have any doubts about your selection, run through the paragraph again, this time skimming it, to make sure you have the correct idea. Remember, though, that you cannot always find it in a few exact words; you may have to rephrase the idea in your own words (which is a good practice anyway) to have it straight.

Consider next how you find the ideas of larger scope than those in each paragraph, that is, the main ideas of sections and chapters. If you did your surveying well, before you read the chapter and as you went along, you probably have a good general idea of what each section is about. In addition, however, authors usually devote certain paragraphs near the beginning and the end of each section to an expression of the main idea of the paragraphs in between. (See, for example, the first two paragraphs under the heading of the present section, Reading with a Purpose.) Any passage of prose has a hierarchy of ideas: a general one for the whole passage, several less general ones under that one, and so on down to the main idea of each paragraph.

Most students read their assignments at least once, which should be enough to spot the main ideas, but somehow many of the ideas are not recognized when they are read. Almost any student, if he reads to get main ideas, can improve enormously his understanding of what he reads and consequently raise his grades on examinations. In addition, reading to get the main ideas is essential to good outlining, for an outline consists of the main topics and ideas of a passage. And outlining, as we shall see in the next chapter, is an invaluable device for learning and reviewing a subject.

**Extracting important details.**  A second major purpose of reading is to locate *important details*. Because students aren't always able to do this, they often think that instructors maliciously look for unimportant or trivial details to ask about in examinations. This complaint, however, is frequently a rationalization for poor reading. So is the frequent excuse "I get the main idea, but I can't remember the details." Although an occasional student may be good at remembering main ideas without the important details, most students are as bad at one as they are at the other because they have not learned how to pick out either. Actually, the main ideas go hand in hand with the important details; one without the other is a structure without supports. The trouble is that each has to be recognized for what it is and not be confused either with the other or with more trivial matters.

What is an important detail? It is the basis for the main idea. Usually it is a fact or a group of facts. It is a fact, though, that is relevant to the main idea. It may be a case in point, an example of the main idea; this is fairly common

in textbooks. It may be the proof that makes the main idea worth believing or accepting. It may merely pin down the main idea to something more concrete. In the case of a narrative, it may be the sequence of events in the story.

What is important is, admittedly, a matter of judgment, and no two people are likely to agree on every item. In most factual textbooks encountered in the natural and social sciences, there is usually at least one important detail associated with every main idea. If the student looks for it, he's pretty sure to find it. Sometimes there are so many details that it is difficult to pick out the most important one. However, the detail or group of details that is stressed most by the language the author uses or by the space the author gives to it is usually the most important one. Another criterion is how closely the detail is tied to the main idea. Is it the best example of the idea? Is it the best proof of the idea? Or is it just one more example or just one more item of proof or support for the idea? Tested in this way, the important detail or details will usually stand out from the others. And if a student remembers just one important detail for every main idea and gets all the main ideas, he'll probably make an A on the next examination. (See Analyzing Paragraphs on the following page.)

The first time you read a passage, you can concentrate on main ideas, reading and noting as many important details as you can. The second time, you may simply review and check yourself on main ideas but concentrate on spotting and remembering important details. The third and perhaps last time you read it, you can do it to review both.

**Other purposes in reading.**  We have described two principal purposes to have in mind in reading assigned textbook material: to get the main ideas and to learn important details. There are still other purposes you should have in some of the reading you do. We will talk about three.

One is to read for answers to specific questions. We explained in the last chapter that asking questions is essential to effective study.

You must think of the questions as you go along; they are suggested to you by headings and by things you read. Then, as you find the answer to one question, this in turn raises questions to guide you as you read farther. Since we've already stressed the value of such questions in studying, we will not dwell longer on it here.

Another purpose you may sometimes have in mind is to *evaluate* what you read. This is most appropriate where you are reading controversial materials, interviews, news stories, and other things that cannot be taken at face value. It is also of varying usefulness in the things you study. When you read a textbook, you can, of course, usually be sure that the writer knows what he is talking about. On the other hand, you'll find that what is said in textbooks, especially of psychology, education, and social sciences, often does not agree with your beliefs or preconceptions. Usually you're wrong and the author is right, and getting your ideas corrected is part of your education.

To make the most of your opportunities, however, you shouldn't take these corrections passively. On the contrary, when you read, read with the purpose of comparing what the book says with what you've thought or believed. When there's a difference, ask right away why the author goes against your views. What is his evidence? Why does he come to his conclusion? Where were you wrong? How wrong?

## ANALYZING PARAGRAPHS

*Here are two passages from an introductory botany book (Edmund W. Sinnott and Katherine S. Wilson,* Botany: Principles and Problems, *5th ed., McGraw-Hill, New York, 1955). In the first of these passages, we have analyzed the words and phrases in the paragraph to illustrate what we have been say-*

*main idea*

*Important details*

*Summary and implication*

*The Plant Cell.* Cells are very small units, the largest being barely visible to the naked eye, and some of the smallest so minute that high powers of the microscope are required to distinguish them. In most plant tissues they vary from approximately 0.1 to 0.01 mm. in diameter, so that from about 15 million to 15 billion would be contained in a cubic inch! An ordinary leaf consists of many millions of cells, and a tree contains countless billions. Bacterial cells are very much smaller, some of them being about 0.0003 mm. in width and close to the limit of visibility by the compound microscope. The largest cells, like those of the pulp of a watermelon, may reach almost a millimeter in diameter. It is hard to think in terms of these very small objects, and one of the difficulties which a botanist must encounter is to carry over into his ordinary experience about plants the facts which the microscope shows him as to their minute structure.

Why? In essence, be critical. Evaluate carefully the author's statements. At the very least, this is a way of keeping yourself alert, of picking out main ideas and important details, and of having them make an impression on you. With this frame of mind, you'll learn more. More important, you will be training yourself for reading, and forming your own opinions about, more controversial material. You will learn "how to use your head," not merely to soak up what a writer says.

Another purpose, finally, to have in reading is to *apply* what you read to your own problems and to the world you live in. The writer doesn't have the space or inclination to point out applications for everything he says. Besides, you live in your own world and have knowledge and experience of your own. In the end, the usefulness of anything you learn depends upon your ability to apply it, and that is your responsibility. If you start thinking about and using what you learn in college, you will later be able to put your college education to much better use.

Applying what you read can be a very personal sort of thing. In the case of this book, we hope it is. It was not written, as textbooks are, to teach either main ideas or details for their own sake. It was prepared to help you. As you've been reading it, your paramount purpose should be to see what applies to you. Some things will and some will not, for every

*ing in the text. The second passage is one for you to practice on. See if you pick out the main idea, important details, and summary. Underline important words and write your diagnosis of them in the space provided in the margin.*

*Photosynthesis.* The primary activity of green leaves is the manufacture of food from certain simple inorganic materials—carbon dioxide and water—by energy derived from light. This process of *photosynthesis* is fundamental in nature, for it is not only a function essential to green plants themselves but one of the utmost importance to animals and man, since it is the sole final source of food in the world. Food is a storehouse of *energy* and of *body-building materials* for living things. In the green parts of plants active, or *kinetic,* energy —in this case the energy of light—is converted into a latent, or *potential,* form, readily available to living organisms for use in maintaining their activities; and in green plants alone are also produced those organic materials out of which plant and animal bodies are constructed. The complex metabolic changes which later take place in the organic world are simply elaborations of the primary products of photosynthesis.

student is different. Each has his specific deficiencies in how to study. We have selected for teaching the things we know many people need to know, but the application is up to you. You must decide or discover how it can be of most help to you. Hence the purpose of reading to apply what you read to yourself is particularly appropriate in the case of reading this book.

## USING YOUR EYES

You know, of course, that you read with your eyes, but you probably don't know just what your eyes are doing when you read. You can't be blamed for that, because the activity of the eyes is so intricate and minute that it can be observed only with special equipment. One apparatus consists of an eye camera so designed that it photographs the stop and go of the eyes when they are trained on a particular passage

of reading. Eye cameras of this kind have been used to record the eye movements of tens of thousands of readers, ranging from very poor ones to very good ones. From the data obtained with these cameras, we know that eye management is pretty important in reading. In fact, you can't hope to be an effective reader unless you learn to use your eyes efficiently.

**Eye pauses.**   When you read a passage of printed matter, your eyes move along the line. You know that, but you may not know that they move in quick jerks with stops in between. In fact, you can't see anything while your eyes are moving. If you did, it would be a blurred swish, like a whip whizzing past. This would probably be so annoying you couldn't stand it, but fortunately you don't have to. The brain has a mechanism for blanking out this part of eye activity. When your eye jumps from one

## EYE MOVEMENTS IN READING

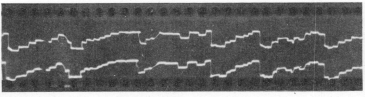

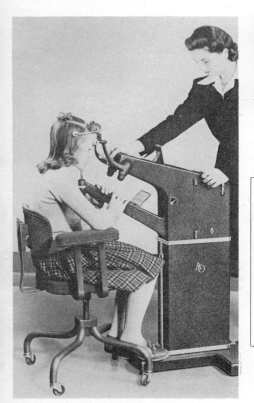

In the picture is an ophthalmograph used for photographing the movement of the eyes in reading. (*American Optical Co.*) The film shows a record of eye movements made with such an instrument. (*New York University Testing and Advisement Center.*) The lines of print show the difference between a good reader and a poor one. Each vertical bar accompanied by a number represents a fixation. The good reader makes relatively few fixations and does not retrace a line.

spot to another on the line, this mechanism keeps the perception of movement from being registered in the brain. Hence you are unaware of the moving blur that you would otherwise see. The important point is that you can perceive words only when your eyes are still, not when they are moving.

Your eye is so designed that it sees most clearly what it fixates, what it is looking directly at. If you look at the word "stop," you see all the letters in it quite clearly. On the other hand, you *can* see the words on either side of it, which are "word" and "you." You don't see them so clearly because they fall on a part of the eye that is not quite so sensitive as the part you are using to look at "stop." The point, though, is that you can see and comprehend these words if you try. The number of words you see at one glance is called your *recognition span*. If you see only one, your recognition span is one word, and that's pretty small. If you see two or three and sometimes more, your recognition span is larger. People with large recognition spans are more likely to be good readers.

There are a number of differences between good readers and poor readers, but perhaps the most important has to do with this matter of recognition span. The poor reader takes in only one word at a glance. Consequently, he is a word-by-word reader. He has to pause for every word on the line. And that's a lot of pauses. For a line like this one, it's ten pauses a line. Obviously, the reader can't read very fast because he is pinned down to each word. Instead of romping down a line, he trudges along it in laborious steps.

But good readers don't do that. They've learned to take in at a glance an average of two words or better. They do this by making use of the words they can see but poor readers ignore. They have practiced at enlarging their recognition span. (A little later in this chapter, we'll show you how you can do that too.) As a result, they don't have to make half the stops the poor reader does, and they whiz down a line twice as fast as the poor reader. Improvement in recognition span cuts reading time in half.

**Saving time.** Good readers also have a couple of other advantages over poor ones. For one thing, they don't dally as long on a pause. There is a limit to the possible brevity of a pause. You can't, on the average, make your eyes stop and start again in less than ⅕ second. So it takes this long to perceive and hence comprehend the words that can be seen in one stop. Poor readers, however, haven't cut their stop time to a minimum. They keep their eyes in one place longer than they need to. The savings to be made here aren't usually as enormous as they are for reducing the number of stops, but they can be appreciable. The good reader, who makes the shortest possible stops, probably saves a third or more of the time spent by poor readers on stops.

Another characteristic of poor readers is that they retrace their steps. Instead of going forward all the time, they often are going backward. Their eyes get part way down a line and then move back a few words to where they were before. (These retracings are called "regressions" or "regressive movements.") This habit occurs partly because poor readers aren't alert when they read and therefore don't comprehend the words they've looked at. They keep missing the meanings when they pause even though they've looked right at a word. When they get farther along in a line or sentence and find they don't understand it, they have to go back and get what they've missed. Partly, though, regressions are just bad habits acquired in sloppy reading. The reader isn't reading with a purpose; he's dawdling. Hence his eyes wander back and forth aimlessly, just as his mind does.

Such regressive movements are unnecessary and wasteful. There are times, especially in very technical reading, when even the best reader has to go back to check something, but the good reader does very little of it. Hence he saves a lot of time by going straight ahead. He also has another advantage: By moving along at a good speed, he goes fast enough not to forget what was at the beginning of the sentence by the time he's reached the end. The poor reader spends so much time meandering back and forth with his eyes that what he has read is pretty stale by the time he has arrived at the end of the sentence. Faster reading, without retracing, actually helps the comprehension of the good reader.

At this point, before we go on to show how you can improve your reading, let us interject an important but neglected precaution. In order to be a good reader, you've got to have *good eyes* or *good corrective glasses*. If you don't have the best possible vision, the words around the word you're looking at will be blurred and you won't be able to perceive them easily. If you haven't had a thorough eye examination recently, better get one. Don't take the slightest chance that your eyes may not be in good condition. By making certain that any slight defects you have are corrected, you will give yourself the opportunity to read at your very best. The dividends you'll get back in time saved and in improved grades will be tremendous compared with the money and time required to look after the matter.

Before reading the next section, we suggest that you take the reading tests, How Fast Can You Read?

## HOW FAST CAN YOU READ?

*Following are two short selections that you can use to get a rough idea about how fast you can read. Before you read them, get a watch or clock with a second hand so you can time yourself. When you are ready to begin, write down the exact time at the head of the passage like this:*

[Hour]___7___:[minute]___23___:[second]___15___

*Then read the passage as rapidly as you can. Do not, however, read so fast that you do not understand and remember what you read because you will want to check yourself on the comprehension test we have provided for each passage. When you are through reading, mark down the exact time at the bottom of the passage. Then go directly to the comprehension test. Do not look back at the passage while taking the test. You should get nearly all the items right on the test (at least nine). If you miss too many items, you have not read carefully enough. You can find a rough index of your speed of reading by checking the following table against the time it took you to read the passages:*

| Passage 1 | | Passage 2 | | Reading speed, |
| --- | --- | --- | --- | --- |
| Minutes | Seconds | Minutes | Seconds | words per minute |
| 6 | 58 | 7 | 5 | 80 |
| 5 | 34 | 5 | 40 | 100 |
| 4 | 38 | 4 | 43 | 120 |
| 3 | 58 | 4 | 3 | 140 |
| 3 | 16 | 3 | 20 | 170 |
| 2 | 47 | 2 | 50 | 200 |
| 2 | 19 | 2 | 22 | 240 |
| 1 | 59 | 2 | 1 | 280 |
| 1 | 44 | 1 | 46 | 320 |
| 1 | 32 | 1 | 34 | 360 |
| 1 | 23 | 1 | 25 | 400 |

## PASSAGE 1

The educational crisis in this country is worsening rapidly. By 1965, enrollment in secondary schools will be more than 70 per cent higher than it was only three years ago. By 1970 we must expect two college students for every one we have today.

This swelling tide of students is matched by an acute and growing shortage of teachers. We are short right now by some 200,000, and of those we have, some 90,000 have failed to pass even the minimum standards for teacher certification. In hundreds of schools important subjects are not taught at all. Forty-six per cent of our high schools offer no foreign language, 23 per cent no physics or chemistry, 24 per cent no geometry. At the college level we shall need to recruit 500,000 *new* teachers in the next twelve years if we are to maintain even present student-faculty proportions.

There is a growing belief that the problem can, in some measure, be relieved by resourceful use of television. So far, experiments in educational TV in this country have been numerically modest (not more than fifty educational institutions are as yet involved), but they have shown that it is more powerful and far more plastic in its uses than many presently suspect. So encouraging have been the results that the Fund for the Advancement of Education has decided to appropriate $968,000 for the most extensive educational TV project yet. Beginning next fall, it will provide regular classroom instruction in eight cities and the states of Oklahoma and Nebraska.

Educational TV can take one of two technological forms (1) open-circuit broadcasting, in which programs are sent out over the air and can be picked up by anyone with a suitable receiver, and (2) closed-circuit broadcasting, in which programs are "piped" to classrooms by coaxial cables and

cannot be received by outsiders.

Some open-circuit educational television originates with regular commercial stations. Philadelphia, for instance, has for nine years broadcast school programs over local commercial outlets. More than 900 television receivers have been installed in the city's classrooms. This year N.B.C. has begun a series of educational broadcasts which go out over its network.

Most open-circuit classroom programs, however, come from stations allocated by the Federal Communications Commission exclusively for use in education. Two hundred and fifty-eight frequencies have been reserved, making theoretically possible a nation-wide network of education stations. Twenty-four such stations are now in operation. There should be thirty before the end of June. The fact that far more are not now on the air is due, partly, to fund-raising difficulties and, partly, to the fact that most of them are in the ultra-high-frequency band to which few receiving sets are as yet adapted. But it is over these reserved frequencies that some of the most striking examples of educational television have been developed.

Pittsburgh's experiment, begun in 1955, has attracted nation-wide interest. Daily teaching by television is conducted in fifth-grade reading, arithmetic and history-geography. Twenty-eight classes in twenty-three different school buildings are involved. Twenty-minute television lessons are given by expert teachers, with varying periods allotted for follow-up by teachers in the classroom. A number of control groups have been established to allow comparison of the television classes' achievement with that of students taught the same subjects under ordinary conditions.

**Time finished.** _____:_____:_____

(*From Charles A. Siepmann, "The Case for TV in Education,"* The New York Times, *June 2, 1957. By permission of the publisher.*)

## COMPREHENSION TEST ON PASSAGE 1

*Mark each statement either true or false.*

_____ 1. By 1970, we must expect five college students for every one we have today.

_____ 2. The present teacher shortage is about

200,000.

_____ 3. Forty-six per cent of our high schools offer no foreign-language courses.

_____ 4. About one hundred educational institutions are now involved in educational TV.

_____ 5. The Fund for the Advancement of Education supports most of these projects.

_____ 6. Some open-circuit educational TV originates over commercial stations.

_____ 7. The Federal Communications Commission has reserved over 200 frequencies for educational TV.

_____ 8. Nearly all the frequencies reserved for educational television are now in use.

_____ 9. Many educational TV stations are in the ultrahigh-frequency band.

_____ 10. Pittsburgh is conducting daily teaching for second grades by TV.

_____ 11. In the Pittsburgh experiment, provision is made for follow-up by the classroom teacher.

_____ 12. The TV lessons in the Pittsburgh experiment are about twenty minutes long.

*The key for scoring the questions above is as follows: (1) F, (2) T, (3) **T**, (4) F, (5) F, (6) T, (7) T, (8) F, (9) T, (10) F, (11) T, (12) T. You should have gotten at least nine right; otherwise, you read the passage too rapidly for adequate comprehension.*

## PASSAGE 2

**Starting time.** _____:_____:_____

If ever there was a medical misnomer it is "normal vision." "Normal vision" is absolutely abnormal, a state of theoretical perfection so rare that it is enjoyed by fewer than 2% of all adults. And even this 2% can be sure of losing it as they grow older. All other people see the world in various degrees of fuzziness and distortion, a situation to which many of them have become so accustomed that anything else would seem intolerable. As a result, many eye doctors, in prescribing glasses, avoid giving patients "normal vision" for fear of the unsettling effect it might have.

This odd circumstance does not keep people from trying to improve their eyesight. It is an axiom among eye doctors that sooner or later everyone needs glasses. In the U. S. alone, some 75 million people wear these visual crutches and spend $300 million on them every year.

As early as the 13th Century it was decided that optical glass lenses were the best means of correcting the minor defects of ordinary vision. During the next 700 years nothing happened to change this basic medical belief. The only widely accepted improvements have been purely technical ones: more accurate ways of measuring eye deficiencies, better methods for grinding finer lenses and, recently, contact lenses, which fit directly over the eyeball.

Most of the nontechnical departures from the eyeglass tradition have been proposed by eccentrics or other personalities who had little stature and less acceptance among recognized medical authorities. The most recent such assault on eyeglasses has been launched by advocates of "visual training."

This is a radical theory of exercising the visual skills which most medically trained eye specialists, or ophthalmologists, deplore but which is finding increasing acceptance among optometrists, the non-medical practitioners who test eyesight and prescribe accordingly.

The following article deals not with diseases of the eye but with ordinary, imperfect vision—the kind that 98% of all people have. Anyone with poor eyesight, which means almost everybody, should understand how the eye works and how its shortcomings can best be corrected.

Understanding the process of vision is no simple matter. The human visual system is an amazingly complicated, self-focusing, twin-barreled camera designed to provide instantaneously developed movies in natural color and 3-D. This is accomplished by two fixed lenses, two adjustable lenses, two film plates no larger than teaspoons, and an immensely complicated series of nerve relays which provide a mental image of whatever is being looked at.

The front of the eye, a curved layer of transparent protein called the cornea, is a powerful fixed lens comparable to that in a box camera. In the act of seeing an object, the cornea refracts, or bends, the incoming light rays, condensing the image and directing it through the pupil. The colored area around the pupil is the iris, which contains small muscles that enlarge the pupil in dim light and contract it in bright light.

Directly after passing through the pupil, the light rays are dealt with by a remarkable apparatus called the crystalline lens. Through automatic adjustments known as "accommodation," this lens changes thickness and curvature to focus the image on the back of the eye, the retina. There the focused light rays activate six million nerve end- ings responsive to color, brightness and detail and 120 million other nerve endings sensitive to motion and dim light. These serve as the eye's photographic film.

**Time finished.** _____:_____:_____

*(From Richard Carter, "The Unending Search for 'Normal' Vision," Life, May 27, 1957. By permission of Time, Inc.)*

## COMPREHENSION TEST ON PASSAGE 2

*Mark each statement either true or false.*

_____ 1. Normal vision is enjoyed by fewer than 2 per cent of all adults.

_____ 2. Many eye doctors in prescribing glasses avoid giving patients normal vision.

_____ 3. It is an axiom among eye doctors that sooner or later everyone needs glasses.

_____ 4. People in the United States ·spend about 100 million dollars every year on glasses.

_____ 5. In the past 700 years medical opinion about the way to correct vision has changed radically.

_____ 6. "Visual training" has more acceptance among ophthalmologists than among optometrists.

_____ 7. The article is going to deal with diseases of the eye.

_____ 8. The cornea is like the fixed lens in a box camera.

_____ 9. Understanding the process of vision is relatively simple.

_____ 10. Before passing through the pupil, the light rays are dealt with by the crystalline lens.

_____ 11. The focused light rays activate 6 million nerve endings sensitive to color, brightness, and detail.

_____ 12. There are 120 million other nerve endings, which also make up the eye's photographic film.

*The key for scoring the questions above is as follows: (1) T, (2) T, (3) T, (4) F, (5) F, (6) F, (7) F, (8) T, (9) F, (10) F, (11) T, (12) T. You should have gotten at least nine right; otherwise, you read the passage too rapidly for adequate comprehension.*

## HOW TO IMPROVE
## YOUR READING

With some knowledge of how your eyes serve you in reading, you are in a position to improve your reading. We shall first give some general guidance for better and faster reading and then prescribe specific things you can do to improve.

**Stop talking to yourself.** Probably the reason many people read word by word is that they first learned to read out loud. Children who are just learning to read do this, and it helps them to get started. Later, of course, they are taught to read silently, but they often do this by talking to themselves. They continue to move their lips when they read and go through all the motions of oral reading without making any noise.

You often can tell whether a person is still talking to himself by whether or not he moves his lips. If he does, it is a sure sign that he is a slow reader; if a person reads at the same rate he talks, he is reading far more slowly than he can and should. Ordinary speech is delivered at a rate of 100 to 125 words a minute. Good readers should read at 200 or more words on difficult textbook material and up to 600 words a minute on easy, storylike material. Nobody can make this speed moving his lips. If you are a lip mover, you've got to get out of the habit.

To develop the ability to read without moving your lips, there are two things you can do: At first, you can place your finger on your lips. This not only tells you when you are moving your lips, thus drawing your attention to your fault, but also acts as a brake on them. It keeps them from moving as they do in talking. The best cure, however, is to practice rapid reading. Try to read so rapidly that there isn't time to move your lips. This advice, admittedly, is a little circular: We want you to stop moving your lips so you can read faster, and we advise you to read faster in order to stop moving your lips. Nevertheless, by deliberately trying to read faster, you can break loose from the lip-moving habit. After you've done that for a while, you'll find you can read faster without its being so much effort.

**Read "thought units."**   Another way to improve your reading is to concentrate on thought units. Though the unit out of which sentences are built is the word, words group themselves together into larger units. These thought units are the more natural units for comprehending the meaning of a sentence, for it is possible to take in each thought unit at a glance.

What is a thought unit? A noun and its modifying adjective. A verb and its qualifying adverb. A prepositional phrase. A relative pronoun and its associated verb. The article together with the noun or adjective it precedes. These are the major thought units in a sentence. For example, in the last sentence, the major thought units might be broken down as follows: "These are—the major—thought units—in a sentence." Each pair or group of words belongs together, and the good reader takes in each group at a glance. You don't have to read every word in that sentence; you can take it in four gulps.

It's not necessary to know precisely what a thought unit is to be able to attend to them. In fact, what it is depends on the difficulty of the

material and how familiar you are with it. The first time you read relatively difficult, unfamiliar material, you may have to take it in rather small units. On rereading the same material or on reading something you already are fairly familiar with, you can group more words into each thought unit. A good reader averages close to two words in a unit for difficult material, and three or more for very easy material. We say "averages" because all units are not the same length. Sometimes the unit is only one word, more often it is two, and sometimes it is three or four. The important point is to try to read more than one word at a time and to do it in terms of the natural grouping of words into thought units.

**Practice reading faster.**   Getting rid of lip movements and concentrating on thought units will not by themselves get you to read appreciably faster. They'll only help. The only sure way to improve your reading speed is to practice fast reading and to practice it so faithfully and for so long that it becomes an ingrained habit. You cannot practice in fits and starts because you'll relapse, in between, into your old habits. You've got to have a systematic program and one that you do not interrupt until you really have mastered the art.

First of all, you should devote a special period every day to training yourself in fast reading. This can be at any time, so long as you can count on it and don't run the risk of having other activities interfere with it. We suggest, however, that it be just before you go to bed. This is a time of day you can count on. It's a time, presumably, when you've finished your studying and can concentrate on something else for a while. It's also a good time for doing a little extra, unrequired reading. Figure on spending about a half hour—certainly no less than ten or fifteen minutes—on your practice in fast reading.

At first choose some light materials that are relatively easy, the kind you might do for the fun of it, for example, *Life* magazine or *Reader's Digest*. The latter is particularly good because it contains many short articles, each of which can be read in a few minutes, and because its pages are uniform enough to tell quickly how many words you have read. A full page of *Reader's Digest,* at this writing, usually contains about 500 words, but you should make allowances for illustrations or other material not part of the text. You had also better check this in case *Reader's Digest* subsequently changes the size of its pages, lines, columns, or type face.

Select an article that interests you. Get a watch or clock that has a second hand and note the time to the second when you start reading it. Read as rapidly as you can and still get the meaning of what you read. When you have finished it, note the time again. Subtract the first time from the second, and divide the number of words by this result to get your rate of reading in words per minute; record it in the chart provided for the purpose. To make sure your comprehension hasn't suffered, ask yourself what you have read; then run back through the article to see that you have gotten all the main ideas and important details. If you have missed any of them, you've probably been reading too fast for your *present* reading ability. Don't let this bother you. Keep on trying to read fast. Only try at the same time to concentrate on getting the main ideas and important details.

If you are using *Reader's Digest* or something like it that has rather short articles, you can probably read three or four articles each night. Time yourself on each one, and record your rate in words per minute. Continue doing this each night for a couple of weeks, trying to pick out articles that are about the same in difficulty from night to night. Practicing on easy material is the best way to break away from your old habits of reading everything at the same speed.

After practicing nightly on reading such easy material, you ought to reach some maximum rate of reading speed within a couple of weeks. You'll be able to tell this from the records you keep of your reading rates. This is probably not the best you can do after you have become an accomplished reader, but it is good enough for the time being. Then it is time to start practicing on material that is more difficult, some-thing that is more like the textbooks you study.

At this stage, we suggest you turn to periodicals such as *Saturday Review, The Atlantic* monthly, or *Harper's Magazine.* These contain interesting and informative articles; yet the style of writing is more challenging. The words are bigger, the sentences longer, and the content more complicated. The level of difficulty is more like that of your textbooks. We suggest that you provide yourself with several copies of one of these magazines and continue your nightly exercises by reading articles in them. Count all the words on one typical full column or page of text so you'll know how many words there are on a page. From this you can easily estimate the number of words on other columns and pages broken up with titles or other material. Then continue your reading as you have before, trying to read as rapidly as possible and keeping track of your speed.

At the same time you are carrying on these nightly reading exercises, you should, of course, be trying to read your regular assignments more rapidly. We suggest separate exercises so that you can have a regular time of day to train yourself and so that you can follow a plan of reading material at about the same level of difficulty. The primary purpose, though not the sole purpose, of such exercises is to help you study more effectively. Hence you should waste no time applying your improved reading skills to your regular studies. In fact, in so far as possible, you should consciously attempt to read faster and faster every time you read anything, no matter what it is.

In reading your study assignments faster, remember that reading speed varies a lot with the kind of material you are reading. You should read most rapidly in history, literature, and philosophy—those things that are most story-like and where main ideas are the important things to get. More technical material that is phrased rigorously and contains many important details must be read more slowly. For example, if you are reading directions in a laboratory manual for doing an experiment, you should read the specific step-by-step instructions very slowly, making sure not to miss any

## RECORD OF PRACTICE IN READING

*Use this chart to keep track of your progress in your daily practice in reading faster. For instructions see text (to find reading rate, multiply the number of pages by the number of words per page and then divide by time).*

| Magazine or book | Pages | Time | Rate |
|---|---|---|---|
|  |  |  |  |
|  |  |  |  |
|  |  |  |  |
|  |  |  |  |
|  |  |  |  |
|  |  |  |  |
|  |  |  |  |
|  |  |  |  |
|  |  |  |  |
|  |  |  |  |
|  |  |  |  |
|  |  |  |  |
|  |  |  |  |
|  |  |  |  |
|  |  |  |  |
|  |  |  |  |
|  |  |  |  |
|  |  |  |  |
|  |  |  |  |
|  |  |  |  |
|  |  |  |  |
|  |  |  |  |
|  |  |  |  |
|  |  |  |  |

detail. You will have to judge for yourself how fast you can go, but you must expect to read different things at different speeds.

Your objective, of course, is to accomplish your reading purpose at the greatest possible speed. That is to say, you must make sure to comprehend what you read and not sacrifice comprehension for speed. If you try to push yourself too fast, you will undoubtedly lose something in comprehension. This is no reason, though, to lapse back into habits of word-by-word reading. You might slow down a trifle because you cannot increase your reading speed all at once. It has to be done gradually, just as a typist or stenographer gradually increases the number of words she can get down. But make sure to go as fast as you possibly can and still comprehend what you are reading. If it turns out that you are going too fast, you can always reread the material again at your top speed to glean what you missed the first time. This will prove a lot more efficient than continuing to trudge along at your old rate.

We should like to insist, in case you have any doubts, that these instructions for reading faster actually do work. It is hard to get data on people who learn by themselves to read faster, for we usually cannot measure them before and after self-training. There are, however, hundreds of cases in which students, after following the advice given here, have reported that they have greatly increased their reading speed, usually by 50 or 100 per cent. In courses that have been given to thousands of college students, business executives, and other persons, nearly everyone has improved some, and the average improvement has come close to doubling the previous reading rate. People in such courses naturally have the advantage of being prodded by the instructor and paced by the course. Yet they still must train themselves. Only by practicing outside the class what they have been instructed to do in class and in books do they actually improve. You can do the same thing!

## BUILDING A VOCABULARY

If you want to be a top-notch student, you must pay attention to another important but sadly neglected matter, your vocabulary. Many tests of students at various levels, including the college level, indicate that good students almost always have a better working vocabulary than poor students. Good students not only can recognize and define more words than poor ones but also can discriminate meanings of words. This helps them read faster because they perceive the meanings of words at a glance, without thinking, and they end up comprehending much more of what they read. Hence part of learning how to study and to read faster is to become a master of the words you read. There are several ways to do this.

**Pay attention to new words.** The first is to look and listen for new words. When you see a new word or encounter one that is only vaguely familiar to you, don't pass it by, thinking you can get along without it. That's not only

## WHAT YOU CAN LEARN FROM A DICTIONARY

*Here is a reproduction of the entry for "memory" in* Webster's New Collegiate Dictionary. *Besides giving pronunciation, the entry gives part of speech (n. = noun) and etymology (OF. = Old French; fr. L = from Latin), then a series of definitions, and finally under synonyms (Syn.) a number of words with meanings that are similar to, but not identical with, those of "memory." Reading and studying carefully this one entry can teach the correct use of a half dozen words. (By permission. From* Webster's New Collegiate Dictionary, *copy-* right 1949, 1951, 1953, 1956, by G. & C. Merriam Company.)

**mem′o·ry** (mĕm′ō·rĭ), *n.; pl.* **-RIES** (-rĭz). [OF. *memoire, memorie,* fr. L. *memoria,* fr. *memor* mindful.] **1.** The power, function, or act of reproducing and identifying what has been learned or experienced; the faculty of remembering. **2.** Commemoration; remembrance; as, in *memory* of youth. **3.** The sum of what one can remember; as, a richly stored *memory.* **4.** A character or conduct, etc., as preserved in remembrance, history, or tradition; as, the war became only a *memory.* **5.** The time within which past events can be or are remembered. **6.** Any particular act or experience of remembering; as, absorbed in *memories* of childhood; also, the thing or things remembered.
**Syn.** Memory, remembrance, recollection, reminiscence mean a remembering or being remembered. **Memory** applies chiefly to the power or function of remembering, esp. what has been experienced or learned; **remembrance**, to the act or process of remembering or to the fact of being remembered; **recollection** adds the implication of bringing back to mind that which is not clear in all of its details; **reminiscence**, of remembering incidents, experiences, etc., from a remote past, such as of one's childhood, in old age.

laziness, it's sheer suicide as far as study is concerned. The meaning of a whole sentence may hang on the new, unfamiliar word. And this may be the sentence with the main idea or an important detail. If that's not true in this case, still the new word may turn up somewhere else as a key word in an idea or detail. And if you are going to read efficiently, you need to know well all the words you read, whether they are key words or not. So cultivate new words. Use them as steppingstones to better reading and understanding.

Once you've spotted a new word, an old word in a new context, or a word you think you know but are not sure of, the first thing to do is look it up in a dictionary. In brief, *get the dictionary habit*. Have a good dictionary handy at all times when you study, and don't be lazy about using it. Once you understand the meaning of a new word, it's part of your personal property and can be yours to understand and use. If you're a poor student, you particularly need to get the dictionary habit, but good students ought to have it too. Accomplished writers, who probably have a better command of English than most people, usually have half a dozen dictionaries for different purposes within arm's reach. They're always looking up new words and even words they've been using all their lives, simply to sharpen their use of these words for particular purposes.

**Use new words.**   Besides looking up new and vaguely understood words in the dictionary, you can take steps to incorporate them into your working vocabulary. It's a good idea to write down any of these words on a card or piece of paper kept for the purpose. During the course of any day in which you are reading two or three hours, you can probably compile a list of several dozen words. If you don't have a dictionary handy when you first encounter them, you can take the first opportunity to look them up. If you do look them up, write them down anyway. Then at the end of the day or at some convenient time, review them to make sure you know what they mean. If you are not certain, look them up again to refresh your

memory. After this review, you can throw the list away.

In building your vocabulary this way, however, you must bear in mind the difference between general words and technical words. General words are most commonly found in literature and history and in newspapers and magazines to describe and interpret things of general interest. They're in the dictionary. Technical words are those used to express concepts, laws, and the special meanings of a particular subject. You'll find plenty of them in natural sciences like biology, chemistry, and physics but also a good many in other subjects, including literature, languages, history, and the social sciences. You won't find most technical words in your ordinary desk dictionary, at least not until they have become so prominent and important in everyday affairs that they should be known by any educated person. (Then they become general words.) Of course, you will be able to look up a great many more technical terms in an *unabridged* dictionary—a book that has a lot of diverse information other than that pertaining strictly to definitions—but the size and cost of such a book usually make it more suitable for the library than for a student's desk.

Textbook writers are supposed to give you a definition of a technical word when they first introduce it. That's one way of finding out what they mean. Sometimes the writer forgets to do that, or he assumes you already know it because you are supposed to have had it in your previous preparation. Or perhaps he did and you missed it, only to run into the word later in the book. In any of these cases, first try the book's glossary if it has one; if not, use the book's index, looking for the word and the sub-entry under it called "definition" or, in lieu of that, any extended discussion of the particular word.

If this doesn't get you a good definition of the word, try one of your more elementary textbooks in the same subject, again using the index to find the word. If you're still unenlightened, try any special dictionary in the subject. There are one or more dictionaries for almost all technical subjects, and you usually can find them in your library by looking up the subject, for example, psychology, chemistry, or economics, and then scanning the cards for "dictionary" or by doing the reverse, looking first for "dictionary" and then for the subject.

Some textbooks have a glossary in the back. This is a dictionary of important terms used in the book. Don't neglect it. The author went to a lot of trouble to prepare it just so you could easily find the correct definitions of the technical terms used in the book.

The importance to effective study of learning technical terms cannot be stressed too much. In some courses, half or more of the subject matter is either a matter of technical terms or can be mastered by knowing these terms. Topnotch students almost always have some way of listing and studying such terms. Sometimes they have a separate place in their notebooks just to enter technical terms as they are encountered in the course. Sometimes they merely underline the words in their notes. However they do it, they make sure to have a pretty complete list of the terms, to know their meanings, and then to review them systematically before an examination. You should do that too.

**Dissect words.** You can do much to develop your mastery of word meanings by paying attention to the structure of words and their history. The English language, and particularly the part of it derived from Latin, is built of certain elements. These are compounded in various ways to make the words we now use. In general, the elements are of three kinds: prefixes, suffixes, and roots. Each of these has a meaning that runs through all the words in which it is used. If you know Latin (and this is one of the best reasons for knowing it), you can translate each element into English, put the elements together, and have a pretty good idea of what the word means. Even without a knowledge of Latin, the meanings of the elements are constant enough for you to learn from the English alone.

In a separate table, we have given some of the more common prefixes and suffixes. Study the meaning of these, and then when you en-

counter a new word, try to figure it out from your knowledge of these prefixes and suffixes. We have also provided a brief list of fairly common root words. If you can recognize the prefixes and suffixes, you can pull the word apart and bare the root word. This, you'll find, is usually familiar to you. Then you can put the three meanings together to obtain the "translation" of the whole word. We should warn you, though, that this process doesn't always give you the precise meaning of words. That often has been modified through usage. Translating the elements only helps you fix the meaning of the word or to make sense of it in terms of how it came about historically.

Another way to understand words better is to use a historical or etymological dictionary. This is a dictionary that breaks words down into their elements, much as we have described in the process above, and then shows you the original meanings of these elements. Such a dictionary also frequently tells you when the word was first used in the English language and

## COMMON PREFIXES AND SUFFIXES

*The following prefixes and suffixes occur frequently in English words. **All are** listed and defined in* Webster's New Collegiate Dictionary *and in many other dictionaries. You can help yourself build a bigger vocabulary by looking up their meanings and writing them in the space provided.*

|  | Meanings |
|---|---|
| **Prefixes:** |  |
| ab-, abs-, a- |  |
| ad-, a- |  |
| be- |  |
| bi- |  |
| co-, com-, con- |  |
| de- |  |
| dis- |  |
| en- |  |
| ex- |  |
| in-, il-, im-, ir- |  |
| non- |  |
| pre- |  |
| pro- |  |
| re- |  |
| sub- |  |
| un- |  |
| **Suffixes:** |  |
| -able, -ible, -ble |  |
| -al |  |
| -ant |  |
| -ent |  |
| -est |  |
| -ful |  |
| -ing |  |
| -ity |  |
| -ive |  |
| -ize |  |
| -less |  |
| -ment |  |
| -ous |  |

## SOME COMMON LATIN AND GREEK ROOTS

*The accompanying list, consisting of ten Latin verbs and two Greek words, provides roots for 2,500 or more English words. (After S. Stephenson Smith,* The Command of Words, *Crowell, New York, 1935, p. 67.)*

| Root word | Meaning |
|---|---|
| capio | take, seize |
| duco | lead |
| facio | do, make |
| fero | bear, carry |
| grapho | write |
| logos | word, speech, knowledge, thought |
| mitto | send |
| plico | fold |
| pono | place |
| tendo | stretch |
| teneo | hold, have |
| specio | observe, see |

what it meant at that time. A good example of such a dictionary is the *Oxford Universal Dictionary*. If you are not familiar with it, you'll probably find one in your college or local library. Spend a half hour with it, looking up any words that interest you. You'll be surprised at how interesting it is, for every word has a history and a story behind it. You'll enjoy learning about them while you make progress building your vocabulary.

# FIVE

# TAKING

# NOTES

**Disorganized notes.**  Some students grab any pieces of paper that happen to be handy, large or small, lined or unlined, punched or unpunched. After scribbling their notes on such odd bits, they stick them into their book, throw them into a folder, or just let them lie around on the desk. Later on, when an examination draws near, the student with such habits searches frantically for his notes. He forgets where he has put them, and if he finds them, he can't recognize them because they are unlabeled. Eventually, he may round them up and put them in some kind of order, but he has lost a lot of valuable time in the process. Then, because the notes are on varying sizes of paper, he can't run through them easily to find what he wants.

There's another kind of student who is serious about note taking and who consciously sets out to keep good notes. He goes to the bookstore and buys a set of bound notebooks. He writes assiduously in them, page after page, as though he were writing a daily journal. Everything goes into his notebook just as he does it. Though such a student is not nearly so badly off as the fellow who takes notes hit or miss on odd bits of paper, he still has trouble with his arrangement of notes. His lecture notes on one subject are followed by textbook notes on a quite different subject because that's the order in which he took them. If he rewrites his lecture notes, as is often necessary, his revised notes appear several pages away from the original notes in the first space that is available. As a consequence, this fellow doesn't have anything in a logical sequence, and he's forever

I T's HARD TO SAY what handicaps students most in their attempts to do college work. A schedule of work, proceeding according to a plan of study, reading with a purpose, and reading rapidly are all important assets. So too are some other matters, and one of them is taking, keeping, and using good notes, both on assigned reading and on lectures. In talking to hundreds of students who have done badly on their examinations, we have found that one of the most frequent and obvious deficiencies in their study methods has to do with their note taking or lack of it. That's the reason we are devoting a chapter to this aspect of how to study.

## HOW TO KEEP NOTES

First of all—and not by any means trivial—are the problems of what kind of notebook to have and how to arrange notes in it.

leafing back and forth trying to find what he's after.

**The well-kept notebook.** The remedy for both these ills is to use a *loose-leaf* notebook, the kind with three rings, which permits pages to be quickly shifted around or discarded if need be. You should set up such a notebook with distinctive tabular dividers, one for each subject you are taking, and plainly write or print each subject on the tab of the divider. At the end of the book, keep a liberal supply of clean ruled paper. Always make sure to use the kind of paper intended for the notebook. Keep the notebook with you whenever you go to class or study. Make it a constant companion during your class and study hours. Then you'll always have all your notes, and they can be kept in order with no trouble at all.

Probably the best size for such a notebook is "letter" size, the one that takes pages about 8½ by 11 inches, such as people use in typewriters or for regular business correspondence. This allows plenty of room for all kinds of notes, and it usually will accommodate all the notes you take in a semester or term.

Since your notebook should get a lot of hard wear, don't skimp when you buy it. Pay a little more, and get one with the sturdiest possible binder. The flimsier ones are likely to fray and even lose their covers before you get through a term.

A couple of other words of advice about how to keep notes: Start your notes for a new chapter on a new page. Similarly, start those for each lecture on a new page. By "lecture," however, we don't necessarily mean class hour. Lecturers seldom stay on their planned schedule, and even if they do, they sometimes devote more than one hour to a lecture. Rather, by lecture we mean a topic that corresponds more or less to a chapter in a book. Usually you can tell when a lecturer finishes one topic and starts another even if he is otherwise not easy to take notes from. By starting each chapter or topic on a new page, you can save time later in getting your notes into any order you want and in rewriting them when that is necessary.

Also be sure to *label* each set of notes. For class notes, put down at the top of the page the date and then a brief statement of the topic. For textbook notes, put down the number of the chapter (or group of pages) and the title of the material. It is even desirable to do this for every single page of notes (just as books have running heads at the top of pages) so that you can always tell at a glance what the notes are about.

Make certain too to keep *all notes* in your notebook. If, for any reason, you are caught without your notebook and take notes on separate sheets of paper, see to it that they are entered in your notebook at the very next opportunity. Also each time you go to class or study a particular subject, make sure that all your notes for that subject are arranged in the proper order. It costs you practically nothing to do this, but it will later cost a lot of time and confusion if you don't.

## UNDERLINING AND OUTLINING

### TEXTBOOKS

Many students don't take notes on their textbook reading. They merely read and underline passages in the book. Underlining has its place, but it is no substitute for the tremendous value

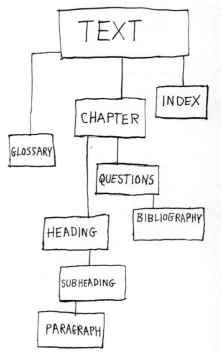

of separate outlined notes kept in a notebook. We'll consider first in this section when and what to underline and then the what and how of outlining.

**Underlining.**    The typical practice of the poor student is to sit down with a chapter in front of him, read away rather listlessly, and then, when he thinks he sees something important, put a line under the prominent words.

He does this without surveying the chapter or asking questions. The result is a hit-or-miss selection of passages, one that represents what interests the student most or seems to him, without any very good basis for judging, to be important. Unfortunately, he is then stuck with what he's done. He thinks he has underscored the important points and uses them later as he studies for an examination. He will have missed many of the really important points and selected others that aren't. In reviewing he doesn't think to check his underlining to see whether it is right; and even if he does, he finds it unfeasible to erase lines and put in others, especially if he has underlined in ink, as so many students foolishly do. When he comes to the examination relying on his poor underlining, he's studied many of the wrong things.

Incidentally, the fact that so many students underline too indiscriminately and in ink is important to consider in buying a used textbook. If you are buying a secondhand book, insist on getting one that has not been underlined; otherwise, buy a new one, for the handicap of someone else's distracting and misleading underlining is far too serious to be worth the small amount you save by purchasing a used book.

Now, as we said, underlining has its place, but it must be done wisely, at the right time, and according to a plan. The plan is this: First you must survey a chapter, and then you ask yourself questions about it and try to answer these questions as you read. In this first reading, it is best not to underline. As your questions are answered or as you think you spot main ideas and important details, put a check mark or a bracket in the margin next to the

seemingly important lines. The next time you read, read for *main ideas* and *important details* and for *technical* terms. It is these you want to underline.

Even on the second, careful reading, don't underline the sentences as you read them. Underline only after you have read one or two paragraphs at a time. Then go back and decide exactly what it is you are going to underline. As a guide, use the check marks or brackets that you made previously. If these now don't seem like the most important points, feel free to change your mind. In any case, select with care what you underline only after you have read all the surrounding sentences.

Then don't underline sentences wholesale. Many of the words in the sentences that contain the main idea or important detail are, as we said earlier, relatively unimportant. Decide which these are and leave them out. Underline only the individual words and phrases that are essential. Underline words so that, when you go back later at reviewing time, you can read merely the underlined words and comprehend immediately the ideas, important details, and definitions.

If you follow these rules in underlining, you probably won't underline as much and as unnecessarily as many students do. On the average, a half dozen or so words per paragraph will do the trick, though the amount certainly depends on the nature of the material. You will also have underlined the best set of words, and you won't find yourself in an examination having "studied the wrong things." Underline lightly. A book heavy with underlining is hard to read and sometimes confusing. A light thin line made with a hard pencil will do.

**Why take notes?**    For most subjects, though possibly not for all of them, you should also take separate notes in outline form of the material in your textbook. There are several good reasons for taking such notes:

In the first place, it forces you to participate actively in the learning process. If you try to write down briefly what the author says, you can't help but make it part of your own mental

# UNDERLINING A TEXTBOOK

*The following passage illustrates the use of relatively little underlining to pick out the main points in a series of paragraphs (from Paul A. Samuelson, Economics: . . . , 3d ed., McGraw-Hill, New York, 1955, p. 43):*

### CAPITAL, DIVISION OF LABOR, AND MONEY     43

to the new or net capital formation, in which current consumption is sacrificed to increase future production.

#### CAPITAL AND PRIVATE PROPERTY

Physical <u>capital goods</u> are important in any economy because they <u>help to increase productivity</u>. This is as true of Soviet communism as it is of our own system. But there is one important difference. By and large, private individuals own the tools of production in our capitalistic system.

What is the exception in our system—<u>government ownership</u> of the means of production—<u>is the rule in a socialized state</u> where productive property is collectively owned. The returns from such real capital goods accrue to the government and not to individuals directly. The government then decides how such income is to be distributed among individuals. The communist government also decides how rapidly resources are to be invested in new capital formation: by how much *present* consumption should be curtailed in order to add to the total of factories, equipment, and productive stocks of goods that are necessary if *future* output is to rise.

<u>In our system individual capitalists earn interest, dividends, and profits</u>, or rents and royalties on the capital goods that they supply. Every patch of land and every bit of equipment has a deed or "title of ownership" that belongs to somebody directly—or if it belongs to a corporation, then indirectly it belongs to the individual stockholders who own the corporation. Moreover, each kind of <u>capital good has a money market value</u>. Hence each claim or title to ownership of a capital good also has a market value. A share of common stock of General Electric is quoted at some certain price, a New York Central bond at another price, a mortgage on a house is valued at some amount, the deed to a house and lot is appraised by the real-estate market at some given level, etc.

Clearly, in taking a census of the nation's total capital, <u>we must avoid fallacious double counting</u>. Nobody could be so foolish as to declare that his total capital was $20,000 if he owned a $10,000 house on Main Street and also had under his mattress a $10,000 deed to that house. Nor would three brothers who owned a small corporation manufacturing electric toasters ever be under the illusion that the million dollars of stock of the company could be *added* to the million dollars' worth of capital goods (factory machines, wire, etc.) held by the corporation.

These cases are too simple to give rise to confusion and need not be discussed further at this point. It is enough to point out that the everyday term "capital" <u>has many different meanings</u>. It may refer to a capital good; it may refer to a bond, stock, security or deed, or any document that represents a claim to an income-producing capital good. Often in everyday parlance, it is processes. You can't fool yourself about knowing what you've read. You've got to find the structure of his discourse and pick out the main ideas and important details. And you must learn them—at least temporarily—to get them down on paper. Hence the chances of your remembering what you read are increased manyfold.

A great deal of research, incidentally, proves that we all remember much better the things we actively do than those that we merely experience. That's why recitation is so valuable an aid to study. In fact, taking notes is one way of forcing oneself to recite.

A second important reason for taking notes on reading assignments is that it makes reviewing so much easier and more effective. If you carefully outline a chapter, you reduce to three or four pages what covers twenty or thirty in the book. Now you've got it without all the extra words the author used merely to illustrate or explain his points. If your outline is a good one, most of your review can be simply a matter of making sure you know what is in it. And since you wrote it, the chances that you do know it or can quickly relearn it are good. Then the underlining you've done in the book serves to fill in details and to give you the correct phrasing of the points you have in your notes. Any rereading you do at that point is just to refresh your memory or make clear what your notes mean. You won't get lost in the woods and fail to see the trees.

**Methods of outlining.**    What is the best way to outline? How do you go about outlining? The very first job in outlining is to pick out the structure of the author's outline. If he has used headings liberally, as many textbook writers do, you can get the skeleton of your outline from these headings. Remember, though, that most headings in textbooks are not sentences; they're just a few key words. They're what we call *topical* headings: the kind a person uses who already knows, and knows very well, what he is going to say. The notes an instructor uses for lectures are probably of this kind, for all he needs is a few words to remind him of what he

wants to say next.

A student, on the other hand, must use headings to learn and to remember things not just to remind himself of things he already knows. It is advisable, then, for the student to make sentences out of the textbook headings. Having found the main idea of the section under a heading, he should rewrite the heading so that it contains this main idea. Some students with excellent memories manage to get along without doing this; but unless you know you are one of the few who can, you had better use a sentence structure, not merely topics, in making your outlines.

Once you understand the author's order of headings and can supply more of your own, you should indicate this order in your notes by two simple devices. One is to indent one order under another. The highest order of heading starts at your left margin, the next order is indented under that, the next under that, and so on. Don't indent either too much or too little. If you indent too much, you'll find you often don't have enough space left on a line for writing out your notes. If you indent too little, you won't be able to tell what is indented and you'll get confused about the order of headings. The best amount of indention is two or three letters, or about half an inch.

The other way of indicating structure in your outline is to use a consistent system of lettering and numbering the different orders. There are two or three different ways of doing this, and if you already have one that you use consistently, there is no need to change it. If you don't, we suggest that you use Roman numerals (I, II, III, . . .) for the highest-order headings, capital letters (*A, B, C, . . .*) for the second order, Arabic numerals (1, 2, 3, . . .) for the third order, and lower-case letters (*a, b, c, . . .*) for the fourth order. If you need additional orders, you can use parentheses around Arabic numerals, for example, (1), for the next order, and parentheses around lower-case letters, for example, (*a*), for an even lower order.

If you consistently use both indention and such a system of lettering and numbering, you'll

# OUTLINING A CHAPTER

*Here is an outline of Chapter Three. It illustrates the general form in which outlines of chapters (or lectures) should be written.*

**Date.** October 15

**Source.** *How to Study*, Chapter Three, The Strategy of Study

Good study methods can be summarized under five rules, condensed in the slogan *Survey Q 3R,* which means *survey, question, read, recite, review:*

I. Surveying provides a general picture of what will later be studied in detail.
   A. First survey the whole book.
      1. Read preface, foreword, and other materials addressed to the reader.
      2. Study the table of contents.
      3. Leaf through the book.
         a. Read summaries
         b. Glance at headings and topic sentences.
   B. Before reading each chapter, survey it.
      1. Read over the headings.
      2. Reread the summary.
II. Questions help learning by giving it a purpose.
   A. Keep asking your own questions.
      1. At first write them down.
      2. Later do it mentally after it becomes an ingrained habit.
   B. Use questions asked by the author.
      1. In the textbook.
      2. In a student's workbook if there is one.
III. To read most effectively, you should do the following:
   A. Read actively, not passively, asking yourself periodically what you have learned.
   B. Note especially important terms.
   C. Read everything, including tables, graphs, and other illustrative materials.
IV. Recitation is a well-established aid to learning.
   A. It should be done while reading a book in order to remember what is read.
   B. Amount of recitation depends on kind of material:
      1. Up to 90 or 95 per cent of study for memorizing disconnected, not too meaningful material such as rules, items, laws, or formulas.
      2. As little as 20 or 30 per cent for well-organized storylike material such as literature, history, or philosophy.
   C. Recitation should be done as follows:
      1. Section by section in reading a book.
      2. In general, immediately after first learning.
V. Reviewing consists of the steps above and the following:
   A. Especially resurveying the headings and summaries.
   B. Rereading, but primarily to check yourself on how well you can recite.
   C. It should be done at these times:
      1. Immediately after studying something, when it should be fairly brief and consist mainly of recitation.
      2. Once or twice in between the first and final review, when it should emphasize rereading.
      3. Intensively in a final review in preparation for an examination, when it should emphasize recitation.

have nicely structured outlines in which the relationship of things to each other is easy to see at a glance.

**Content of notes.** What do you put into your notes? We've already said that topical headings should be rephrased to include the main ideas of the sections they head. Beyond that, you should include main ideas and important details at each level of the outline. One system that we recommend is to construct your outline from main ideas at different levels and then add after each main idea, either as additional sentences or in parentheses, whatever important details are relevant. Definitions, which are very important details, can also be inserted in parentheses after you've stated the main idea. Sometimes, of course, a definition *is* the main idea and should be outlined accordingly.

We add one general warning: Write legibly enough to be able to read your notes many days after you've written them. Even people who have a good hand get in such a hurry when they take notes that they later can't read their own scrawl. There's no advantage to hurrying at the sacrifice of legibility, for legible notes are so valuable to you later that the time you take to make them so is fully repaid. If your writing is hard to read anyway (unfortunately this is the case with far too many students), make a special effort to improve it when you take textbook notes. Perhaps by practicing at this time you may learn to write well enough for the instructor to read your writing; you would be surprised to know how many grade points that is worth.

Making outlined notes of textbook material will help you understand what you read and then to know it when examination time comes. There are some kinds of material, however, for which you should not make outlines. You don't do this, obviously, for some stages in learning a foreign language, especially where the job is to learn vocabulary or for the exact translation of a passage. Some textbooks, particularly in the physical sciences, are already in outline form, and it is hardly worth your while to copy an outline from a book. In such cases, you will use techniques other than out-

## THREE WAYS TO SUMMARIZE A STORY

*Here is an account of the same event told in three different ways. Notice how they differ in order, style, and content.*

### The newspaper story

The family of Mr. and Mrs. John Doe of Millvale Road miraculously escaped injury and possible death last night when the frantic barking of the family dog aroused Mr. Doe. A fire had broken out in the basement, filling the house with smoke and fumes. The family escaped through a second-story porch window. James Doe, 8, and Jane Doe, 10, were treated for smoke inhalation at City Hospital. The fire is believed to have started in a defective furnace motor. The interior of the house suffered considerable damage.

### The insurance adjustor's report

The residence at 210 Millvale Road, owned by John and Mary Doe, insured under Policy No. 218956, suffered damages from fire and water incidental to smothering the fire on the evening of 15 June 1957. Damages to the premises, furnishings, and personal apparel insured under the above Policy are appended in Report A. The statement as a result of investigation by the Fire Inspector of the City of Springdale established the origin of the fire as a short circuit in the blower motor of the oil furnace, under service contract held by the Springdale Fuel Company. A detailed report of the condition of the motor is appended in Report B. No personal injuries resulted either due to fire or action of the fire department.

### Mrs. Doe's letter to her mother

Dear Mother,

A terrible thing happened last night. Our house caught on fire! Everybody is safe, and the insurance adjustor tells us the damages are completely covered by our policy. We lost a lot of valuable things, of course, but we thank heaven no one was hurt. We all have Skippy to thank. He woke us up by whining just as the smoke was getting very bad upstairs. We all got out just in time; I think we would have suffocated if we had been much longer. As you can imagine, we are all tired and upset. I'll write details tomorrow.

Love,
Mary

*These versions say somewhat different things, but they also differ in style and individual words. The newspaper account uses words like "miraculously" and starts right out with the rescue by the family dog (dramatized a little by the substitution of "barking" for "whining," which would have been more accurate). The prosaic insurance adjustor mentions first the address and the policy number and then soberly recites the facts of interest to his company. The letter is informal and not well organized; it stresses the personal feelings and condition of the family rather than the facts.*

lining. We shall describe some for the study of foreign languages in a later chapter. Where the book is already practically an outline, you'll do better to emphasize good underlining and to put a lot of emphasis on recitation rather than on outlining.

**Writing summaries.** There are other instances in which you should take notes but not necessarily in outline form. Often, when reading literature, for example, you are not reading for a number of specific points. Rather, you want a synopsis, or summary, or even an interpretation

of what you've read. In this case, your best method of taking notes is to jot down important points as you go along; then at the end you can compose a summary that tells the gist of the story. Consider what interpretation the author is trying to convey about the story he tells. There are many ways of telling a story (see Three Ways to Summarize a Story). Why does the author tell it in the way he does? Is he trying to convey a feel or atmosphere? Is he ironic? Why is he ironic?

There's another occasion too for writing summaries. This is in the case of textbooks that

## A SUMMARY

*To illustrate the writing of summaries, we give below a summary of Chapter Four, Reading Better and Faster. Compare the statements in this summary with the headings and main ideas of the chapter. Also, by referring to the sample outline on page 59, note in what ways a summary differs from an outline.*

Most college students cannot read well; they take too much time and don't learn what they should. By heeding the following points, however, they usually can enormously improve both their speed and their comprehension.

All reading should be done with certain purposes in mind: (1) One is to get the main idea of each paragraph, subsection, and main section. (2) Another is to select important details; these are statements that explain, prove, illustrate, or exemplify the main ideas. Other purposes are (3) to answer questions raised by teacher, author, and student himself, (4) to evaluate the reading in terms of what the reader otherwise knows and believes, and (5) to apply the reading to one's daily life and to his general understanding of the world.

When a person reads, he moves his eyes along in quick jerks with stops in between; all perception occurs during the stops. In order to manage his eyes most efficiently, there are three things to do: (1) increase his recognition span by taking in two or three words at a time, not just one; (2) try not to dally so long on each pause, cutting stopping time to a minimum; (3) keep his eyes moving forward all the time, never letting them wander backward along the line. He should also make sure either that his eyes are good or that he has the proper corrective glasses.

To improve further his effectiveness in reading, he

should practice the following things: (1) reading without moving his lips, for lip moving holds reading rate down to a quarter of what it should be; (2) learning to read in thought units—the natural grouping of words into phrases of two, three, or four words; (3) practicing reading faster by devoting a special period every day to reading exercises, starting out with easy materials and progressing to more difficult materials and keeping a record of his progress in these exercises; (4) in trying to read faster, however, making sure that he comprehends what he reads—comprehension should never be sacrificed for reading speed.

The ability to read rapidly and to remember what is read depends to a great extent on vocabulary. You should constantly strive to build up your vocabulary by stressing the following: (1) Always look and listen for new words—unfamiliar words or words whose meanings are hazy—and look them up in a dictionary. (2) Make a point of using new words at the next opportunity in studying, talking, or writing. Pay special attention to technical terms in textbooks, noting their definitions when they first appear and looking them up in glossaries, dictionaries, or other textbooks. (3) Dissect words into their component prefixes, suffixes, and roots; where possible, look up their history to see how they are derived from French, Latin, Greek, or other languages.

have no summaries at the end of the chapters. Some authors, in fact, do not provide summaries because they think the student will profit most by constructing his own even though he loses the benefit of a summary in surveying the chapter. Hence if your textbook doesn't have summaries, take advantage of the opportunity to learn something by writing your own.

Don't try to write the summary until you've first outlined the material. Then, after reviewing the outline and using it as a guide, write a series of paragraphs, usually no more than one or two pages long, summarizing the chapter. You'll probably make out best if you let each paragraph stand for a major item in your outline. The main idea of a section, in fact, can be your topic sentence. The other sentences in the paragraph can then be the main ideas of the subsections under the main section. Writing such an outline is one form of recitation and has all the attendant benefits we have described. It is also good practice for writing essay-type examinations, where you must organize succinctly the main points on a question or topic.

## TAKING LECTURE NOTES

Most students know they should take notes in class, if only to impress the instructor, but many don't know how to go about it. They take either too many or too few, and they don't take the best ones. Taking lecture notes is an art that must be developed by practice. It requires effort and an alert mind. Also involved is additional work after class to edit and, often, to rewrite the notes. But good lecture and classroom notes can be the key to remarkable academic improvement.

Much of what we have said in the previous section applies to lecture notes as well as to notes made on textbooks. In fact, the whole *Survey Q 3R* plan of study is applicable to lectures, but not in every detail.

**Surveying, questioning, listening.**  Naturally you can't survey a lecture in advance unless the instructor does it for you, which not many do. Many lecturers, however, *do* give something of a preview of what they are going to say. When one does, be on the alert and make notes very rapidly on the points he says he is going to cover. This is the closest thing to a survey you'll get; to make the most of it, refer frequently to your notes on the preview as the lecture proceeds. Thus you'll know what to expect, and you'll have a better idea of what is important and what isn't.

The question part of *Survey Q 3R* is also appropriate in lectures. If possible, before you go to class, think of questions based on your reading of the textbook assignments and on what the lecturer said last time. As soon as you are settled down in your chair, get your notebook ready (see page 55) and put your mind to work on what is going to happen in class. Get to questioning and thinking, and continue doing it throughout class. You're there for a purpose, not to pass the time of day; and the more effort you put out, the more you'll get from class.

In class, of course, you don't read. If you do, you're going to miss a lot. You listen, and you listen hard. Since there are no headings and there is no opportunity to look back to check yourself, you've got to make sure you take in and evaluate everything. Much that the lecturer says will only be in support of his main points and need not be remembered, just as many of the words in a written paragraph are there merely for supporting purposes. But you must listen to it all to tell what is important and what is not.

**Getting the organization.**  Somehow or other you must comprehend and note the organization of what the lecturer is saying. This is equivalent to noting the headings in a book. Only here you must often figure out for yourself what the headings are. Some lecturers use the blackboard to write down the topics they're talking about. If so, fine. It will provide the skeleton for your notes. If not, you must somehow make up or pick out the outline for yourself. Sometimes this is almost impossible, and you will have to write down all that seems to be important and then organize it after class.

Even the most disorganized lecturer, however, gives you many clues to his organization if you will only recognize them and use them. One clue may be the statement "The main point is this: . . ." or "Note this: . . ." or "Remember this: . . . ." Another clue may be the mere repetition of a statement; if the lecturer takes the trouble to say something twice, he must think it's important. Or he may say essentially the same thing in two or three different ways, which is a kind of repetition, and this may be your clue. Changes of pace may also serve as clues. When a lecturer suddenly slows down and says something as though he specially wanted you to get it, his statement is probably important. Or if his voice changes in tone or loudness so as to give his statement emphasis, that signals an important point.

Lecturers have different styles, and they may use any of these clues in any combination. As soon as you begin taking a course, study your lecturer carefully to see what his particular style is and how he gives his clues. For this purpose, it is often helpful to compare notes with a couple of other students and discuss with them the lecturer's style. Another student may pick up clues you don't, and vice versa.

One way or another, you should be organizing what the lecturer says and take notes according to this organization. You do it by trying to identify the lecturer's main points. You look for main ideas and then for important details connected with them, just as you do in textbook reading. If you listen carefully, you'll find that there are paragraphs in his spoken words as there are in a book. Your job is to condense these paragraphs into simple phrases and sentences that include the main ideas and important details. You should do this in words of your own phrasing, not in those of the lecturer, in order to make sure that you really understand what he is saying. On the other hand, if he gives you a technical definition or states something obviously intended to be a precise statement, you should take this down verbatim.

Sometimes it is difficult to organize your lecture notes as you are taking them down and even to be sure all the time what the main points

are. In this case, you are forced to take copious unorganized notes just to keep up with the lecture. Don't do that unless you can't avoid it. In any event, though, don't spend so much time trying to take neat well-organized notes that you lose the point of the lecture. Almost any kind of note is better than none at all. Still, the more organized your notes are, the more useful they will be later on.

The question of how many notes you should take depends somewhat on the individual, how apt he is at spotting main points, and how rapidly he can write. It also depends on the lecturer and how many main points he has. Some lecturers jam a lot into an hour, others relatively little. Some students do their best by taking many notes, and others do just as well by taking rather few. In general, though, it is best to err on the side of taking too many. You can always sort them out and reduce them later. If you take too few, you may never regain what you have lost.

**Reviewing and revising.** Review in the *Survey Q 3R* formula is even more important for lecture notes than it is for reading textbooks. Your lecture notes, unlike your textbook, are incomplete, imperfect, and not so well organized. It is therefore necessary to review them carefully and frequently to recall and recite as much as you can, thus battling the inexorable law of forgetting. Your first review should be right after the lecture or within a few hours of it. At that time much of what the lecturer said is still fresh in your mind, and you can fill in essentials that did not get into your notes. You can even correct errors that crept in by writing something down hurriedly or before you understood it. If you wait too long to review your notes, you may easily wind up saying, as many a student has, "My lecture notes just don't make sense."

It may often pay you to rewrite your lecture notes completely. We don't recommend that you do this needlessly, for you can waste time doing it. Some students manage to get neat well-organized notes and need to do only a little editing, making occasional inserts and cross-outs. Students who aren't in this class may be well advised to rewrite almost all their notes. Even the best students may have to rewrite when the lecturer's style defies all attempts to organize what he is saying while he is saying it. You'll have to decide for yourself when and what you should rewrite. If you suspect you need to, you'd better do it. For if you manage to organize more clearly what you've written, you'll be much better off later. And you'll get some valuable recitation and review in the process.

This is almost all we need say about taking lecture notes except to emphasize that the other things we've mentioned about the *Survey Q 3R* formula are applicable to lecture notes. Do your first review and rewriting shortly after the lecture. Some time later, review your notes fairly lightly again. Then, in the two or three days before an examination, review them thoroughly.

## RESEARCH NOTES

Besides taking notes regularly on textbooks and lectures, you'll have other occasions in your college work to take notes. You'll have outside readings, book reports, term papers, and even research papers to do. Most of these require you to adapt the note-taking methods we have already described, but there are circumstances in which you had better do something rather different.

**Summary notes.**  In most of these special cases, you won't need to outline what you read. The principal exception may be book reports. If you read and report on a book, it may be desirable to make some sort of outline. The outline, however, need not be nearly so detailed as the outlines you make of textbook or lecture material. Rather, your outline should include only one or two orders of heading with their main ideas. What you end up with will look much like any other outline except that it is briefer and less detailed.

For most other situations, your finished notes will be in the form of summaries. While you are reading, you may jot down the rudiments of an outline; but when you're finished, you should take these rough notes as your guide and compose a summary of the principal points in the reading. How lengthy or detailed it is depends on the size of the reading, on what the instructor has suggested you do, and on your purpose in reading. Once you have your summary composed, you can usually throw away your rough, reading notes.

**Use of cards.**  At other times you may do what can be called "research reading." Having a general topic to write on or learn about, you look up a number of books or read a number of different articles in magazines, journals, or other periodicals. We won't discuss just now either how you find the materials you read or how you write a paper based on them, for these matters will be considered in Chapter Eight. For the time being, we're interested only in how you manage your notes for such research reading.

One feature of this kind of reading is that you don't know exactly how much of it you will eventually use until you have finished reading almost all your library-research materials. The topic you had in mind when you started may turn out to be too big, or some of the articles may prove to be too peripheral or unimportant for your purposes. Another feature of research reading is that you don't know either, as you read, just how you will organize your paper. This only begins to emerge when you are close to finishing your reading. And undoubtedly you will not use the articles in your paper in the same order you read them in. Moreover, when you come to write your paper, some articles will be used many times and others hardly at all.

These two points have an important implication: They require that you be able later to organize and reorganize your notes in any sequence that suits your purpose. Consequently, they make it poor strategy to take notes on sheets of paper the way you take lecture or textbook notes. For this purpose, cards are much better materials to use. If you have one

# RESEARCH NOTES

*Here are three cards illustrating notes taken on articles. Note the form of the citations and the kinds of summary written.*

Elder, J., Elder, C., + Bradley, P.B. The effect of
some drugs on the electrical activity of the brain,
and on behavior. J. ment. Sci., 1954, 100, 125-128.

The effects of five drugs were studied in
cats by observing changes in behavior and electrical
activity recorded from electrodes buried in the brain.
The same drugs were also used with human volunteer
subjects and with patients in a mental hospital.
Certain drugs affect certain parts of the nervous
system more than other parts.

---

Dennis, Wayne. Bibliographies of eminent scientists.
Sci. Mon. N. Y., 1954, 79, 180-183.

Evidence is presented for the conclusion that
eminent scientists usually publish an unusual
number of articles, monographs and books. In
general, the greater the number of publications by
a scientist, the higher is his reputation.

---

Milligan, L. H., + Osmanski, J. E. Attitude survey
followed up by "feedback" sessions. Personnel J.,
1954, 33, 92-96.

Supervisory personnel at Crucible Steel Company
were given an opinion survey. This revealed several policies
concerning salary and wage levels, pension plans, etc.,
not liked by the supervisors. The results of the survey
were distributed to all supervisors taking part in the
survey, and in bi-weekly conferences the supervisors
were given explanations of the policies they liked least.
A follow up opinion survey showed that supervisors
now felt more favorably toward the policies they
formerly disliked.

card for each article you read and keep all your notes for the article on this card, you can later shuffle and arrange these cards to have them in any sequence that fits the organization of your paper. People who write textbooks or scholarly articles have this problem on a large scale, often involving thousands of articles, and they almost invariably do all their note taking on cards.

In your bookstore, you can probably find all sizes of card for any purpose. The smallest cards are 3 by 5 inches, the next size 4 by 6 inches, and the largest size 6 by 9 inches. For most purposes, either the 3 by 5 or the 4 by 6 is best. You can't get many notes on a 3 by 5; and since it is best to get all notes on the two sides of a card, the 4 by 6 cards are usually the best bet. You'll want to decide, though, on the basis of the particular job you have to do. The main point is that if you are reading a number of articles, doing research on a topic, you should take your notes on cards, not on notebook paper. It's a good idea, incidentally, to have a card box in which you can file your cards.

**Notes on cards.**   The first thing you put on a card is the *correct* reference. If your source is a book, your reference must consist of the name or names of the author(s), including all initials given on the title page, the title of the book, the place where it is published, the name of the publisher, and its copyright date (not the date of its last printing). Although you may not need it, you should also include the number of pages of front matter, which are indicated by Roman numerals, and the total of the regularly numbered pages. If your source is a magazine or journal, your correct reference must include author(s), title of the article, name of the journal, the year, the volume number, and the pages on which the article begins and ends. Be careful to take down these data without mis-

takes, for you or someone else may use the reference later and rely on its being correct.

The exact way in which you list the above information in a list of references varies from one field to another. Each professional group or sometimes a particular journal has its own customs governing citation. You should follow those accepted in the field you are working in, and the easiest way to determine the customs is to look at the references at the end of the chapters or articles you read. If these don't make the system clear, follow the form of the *World List of Periodicals,* a big book that can be found in the reading room of almost any library. Whatever you do, though, *be consistent* throughout any one assignment or paper.

What kind of notes do you put on your cards? In general, you write brief summaries. What you consider important in the article depends on your purpose in doing the library research and also, of course, on your judgment. Your job is to extract the main ideas and important details that are relevant to your purpose. If you miss some of these the first time you read the article (and even the most accomplished scholars sometimes do), you always have the reference on your card and can go back to look up the article again. Most of the time, though, a thoughtfully written abstract or summary will suit your purpose.

When all your reading is completed, you can run through your cards, making rough notes on a sheet of paper. From these notes you can make up an outline of what you intend to write in your paper. Then, using your rough notes as a key to this outline, you can sort your cards and rearrange them so that they are approximately in the order you want them for your writing job. How you go about this job is something we will consider later in Chapter Seven.

HAVING READ THE TITLE of this chapter, you may say, "Ah, that's what I want to know: how to take examinations." You may even harbor the hope that we know some way to pass an examination without studying for it. That's a bit of magic, however, that no psychologist has yet produced. Nor should he, for the basic purpose of examinations is to measure how effectively you've studied beforehand. If you have already done the things we've outlined to improve your studying habits, you've done most of what is necessary to be ready for examinations. Still, there are a number of pointers that we can give you to bring you to top efficiency in taking examinations.

## PREPARING FOR EXAMINATIONS

The only good general rule for taking examinations is "Be prepared." This means being prepared for the kind and scope of examination you are to take and for all the questions you may be asked, not just some of them. It means having a thorough mastery of your subject matter, not a hazy acquaintance with it, and having it so well organized that you can tap it in any way that is called for. It means being rested, emotionally stable and calm, and in the pink of mental condition. Let's look into these matters in more detail.

**The final review.**  If you've done your studying as you should, preparing for an examination is largely a matter of review. You review the notes you've taken in class and on the textbook, the main ideas and important details

SIX

## TAKING

## EXAMINATIONS

you've underlined in the textbook, and lists of technical words you've acquired as you study. This review should be more intensive than any you've done since you reviewed right after first studying the material. It should, however, be a review and not an attempt to learn things that you should have learned earlier. If just before the examination you are still reading material for the first time and making notes on it, you're already seriously handicapped. You'll be trying to do too many different things at once and in too short a time. Though you *might* be bright enough to scrape through by doing things this way, you'll certainly do a lot better if you've already done your reading and note taking and need only to review.

In some subjects, you may want at this time to make some new notes, especially for the purposes of review. If you have a lot of material to cover and have a great many notes, you can make a set of summary notes in three or four pages that will extract the essence of your more detailed material. In constructing these summary notes, you distill the most important ideas and details from your other notes, referring to the book occasionally to check on a point. You end up with a summary of a summary. In this way, you can make sure of the very important points, you then have something to run over before examination, and you obtain the advantages of additional recitation.

**Scheduling reviews.**   Contrary to what most students do, or think they should do, the period of review before an examination need not be long. For weekly quizzes, it need be no longer than a few minutes; for a midterm hour exam, only two or three hours; and for a final exam, five to eight hours. That's assuming, of course, that all you need to do is review. The periods of reviewing, moreover, should be pretty short, an hour or an hour and a half, interspersed with periods of rest or recreation. If you work too

## SCHEDULE OF REVIEW FOR FINAL EXAMINATIONS

*Plan carefully the time devoted to review for final examinations. Enter the days of the week in the spaces at the top of the columns. Then write in the squares the specific subjects you plan to study each hour of the day. Leave a reasonable time, however, for meals and recreation.*

| Time \ Day | | | | | |
|---|---|---|---|---|---|
| 8:00 | | | | | |
| 9:00 | | | | | |
| 10:00 | | | | | |
| 11:00 | | | | | |
| 12:00 | | | | | |
| 1:00 | | | | | |
| 2:00 | | | | | |
| 3:00 | | | | | |
| 4:00 | | | | | |
| 5:00 | | | | | |
| 6:00 | | | | | |
| 7:00 | | | | | |
| 8:00 | | | | | |
| 9:00 | | | | | |
| 10:00 | | | | | |

hard at reviewing a lot of material, you'll get confused and actually remember less than if you follow a less strenuous schedule.

You should plan definite periods for review in your study schedule just as you schedule your regular hours of study. Find out as early as you can when a quiz or examination is to be given. Then make out a slight revision of your study schedule for the week or two before the examination, writing down particular hours for review. Try not to disturb the hours you'll need to keep up with regular studying for your other subjects. Instead, set aside some of the hours regularly assigned to the particular subject and some of the "optional" hours in your schedule. In addition, you may, if necessary, take a few hours otherwise devoted to recreation, but don't cut into them too deeply. They're necessary to keep you in good shape and to keep you from overdoing the reviewing.

This brings us to another subject on which many students need advice: In the long run, it

## SCHEDULE FOR PERIOD OF FINAL EXAMINATIONS

*When you know your schedule of final examinations, enter it in the chart. After that, enter specific subjects you will review in the hours available. Again, however, make sure to leave time enough for meals and recreation.*

| Time / Day | | | | | |
|---|---|---|---|---|---|
| 8:00 | | | | | |
| 9:00 | | | | | |
| 10:00 | | | | | |
| 11:00 | | | | | |
| 12:00 | | | | | |
| 1:00 | | | | | |
| 2:00 | | | | | |
| 3:00 | | | | | |
| 4:00 | | | | | |
| 5:00 | | | | | |
| 6:00 | | | | | |
| 7:00 | | | | | |
| 8:00 | | | | | |
| 9:00 | | | | | |
| 10:00 | | | | | |

does not pay to go without food, sleep, and a reasonable amount of recreation to "cram" for examinations. Staying up half the night or even all night may seem like the thing to do when you're behind in your work, but you pay (and pay dearly) for it. In the first place, you don't have all your wits about you in an examination; you can't organize material or recall it as well on a written examination, and you're not so sharp in discriminating the right and wrong answers of an objective test. You also must make up later for your lost sleep, with the result that you break up your schedule of work, cut classes, and fall behind in your other work. The whole thing becomes a vicious circle. Once you start cramming for examinations, letting other studies and your sleep get shortchanged, you have to do it more and more and never get out of the circle.

Of course it is the fashion to talk about how much cramming you did, to boast about how little sleep you got and how you lived on coffee and booster pills. Most students do more bragging than cramming, but the fact is that any amount of such frantic, helter-skelter studying is inefficient and harmful. Take the boasting of your fellow students with a bit of skepticism, and organize your own life to be cool, collected, and efficient.

You should therefore do everything possible to live a normal life during times of preparation for examinations. Get your meals, sleep, and recreation and do other studying on schedule. You can and should work a little harder than usual, but don't let it throw everything out of gear. If you've done a reasonable amount of reviewing, a good night's sleep will net you more points on an examination than staying up late trying to learn a little more. In fact, the best advice for reviewing is to review two or three hours the day before, take the evening off, and get to bed early.

**How to review.**    In reviewing for an examination, you should keep rereading to a minimum. Rather, your review should emphasize recitation. In reviewing a chapter, try to recall the main ideas of the chapter without referring to your notes. Then check your recollections against your notes. Under each main heading of the chapter, do the same thing again; try to recall the points under this heading, then check. If there is something you have difficulty recalling or something you don't quite understand, go back to your textbook and reread the passage covering it. That's about all the rereading you should do. If you attempt to do much more than that, you spend so much time rereading that you lose sight of the important points or you skip around so aimlessly that it does you little good.

Another bit of advice is good if you follow it completely; otherwise, it may mislead you. This is to *predict* questions you may be asked on the examination. Ask yourself as you review: "Is this something that could be a question?" "Has this been emphasized?" "How could a question be asked on this topic?" Also take advantage of the clues furnished by instructors. Most of them give some hints directly or indirectly about specific questions they are likely to ask. Such hints may be found in the importance an instructor attaches to certain points he makes or in the time he dwells on a particular topic. They may be contained in advice he gives about studying for the examination.

One way or another, you should be able to spot a great many questions that subsequently appear on the examination. Since you've predicted them, you've rehearsed for them, and you're ready for them. Later, after the examination, if it is not a final, you can study the questions you failed to predict and use your misses as a guide for predicting questions on future examinations.

We must emphasize, however, that this advice can be misleading if you carry it out in the wrong way, that is, trying to outguess the instructor on the questions he'll ask and then studying only the things you think he'll ask. One variation of this faulty approach is to study only the things that appeared on examinations the term or two before. If you thus limit yourself to the few items you guess will be asked, you may luckily hit on some of them, but most of the time you'll miss enough to pull your grade down several notches. Very few instructors are oblivious to this guessing game. Most work pretty hard to ask questions that are not easily anticipated. Therefore, when you predict questions you will be asked, predict all that could be asked, not just a few you hope or guess will be asked. Otherwise you may be saying those famous last words, "I studied the wrong things."

**Types of examination.** Generally speaking, the examinations you'll take in college fall roughly into one of two categories: One is the *objective* examination. This doesn't require you to write anything. All you have to do is decide whether certain statements are true or false, which of several statements is true, or how statements should be matched. Such an examination stresses your ability to *recognize* correct answers, not your ability to recall or organize answers. The other type of examination is the *essay* examination. In this, you must *recall* what you have learned. You are asked a question and must then choose and organize the material you consider to answer it best. In other cases, such as mathematics and physics, you may be given problems to solve. Like essays, problems stress your ability to recall, rather than recognize, information. In between, of course, are other possibilities such as the completion test, in which you merely fill in a word, a phrase, or a brief statement. Again, though these don't emphasize ability to organize a lot of information, they do stress recall.

Should you study differently for these different kinds of examination? The answer is both "yes" and "no." You should prepare somewhat differently for each type but not so differently as many students think. Objective examinations seem easier because they require you only to select (or guess at) the right answer. Consequently, students often don't study as hard for them as for essay examinations. It is just as difficult, however, to make good grades on one type of examination as on the other for the simple reason that all students have the same advantages or disadvantages. On the average, therefore, a student ends up in the same rela-

tive position—and thus usually with about the same grade—on one examination as on the other.

Students also feel that objective examinations tend to emphasize details more than essay examinations do. This feeling, however, is largely an illusion. It's due to the fact that the detailed statements of an objective examination stare them in the face, but the student taking an essay examination rarely realizes just how many details he should have known to write a good examination. If you feel that objective examinations tend to cover trivial points, compare the next such examination you take with the headings and important points in your textbook and notes. You'll find they correspond pretty well, and it is these points you *should* know if you're organizing an essay question. Actually, in both types of examinations, the instructor is trying to test your knowledge of main ideas and important details. You should therefore study these regardless of the type of examination.

The principal difference between the two types is not so much one of details as one of *organization*. You simply don't have a chance to organize your knowledge in an objective examination, and you do on the essay test. Thus it is perfectly clear that you must give more attention to organization when you prepare for an essay test. This means somewhat more recitation to enable you to recall in outline form what you know. On the other hand, don't neglect organization entirely when you study for an objective test. Some of the questions will be so phrased that they will test your knowledge and understanding of the relationships between various parts of the material.

There is no question but that the objective examination puts a higher premium on recognition than on recall. Our memories are such that we all can recognize many things we cannot recall. This fact leads to the conclusion that, in studying for an objective examination, we should try to be ready to recognize points that we wouldn't be called upon to recall in an essay examination. This means that the final review before an objective examination should include more rereading of the text and, particularly, of notes and somewhat less recitation than are appropriate for an essay examination.

Although there are these differences, we must emphasize that you should not go to extremes in your preparation. All reviews should include some rereading and some recitation. You only do a little more of one than the other for one kind of examination. All reviews too should stress knowledge of the main ideas and important details.

**Attitude toward examinations.**   In a moment we will discuss the specifics of taking examinations, but first we ought to say something about emotions and attitudes regarding examinations.

Students tend to think of examinations as among the trials of life, ordeals that can't be escaped and must somehow be survived. They look forward to tests with fear and trembling and often are terribly upset both before and during an examination. This negative, fearful attitude is unfortunately reinforced by the fact that grades depend on exams. The student who is not doing very well can easily feel that the exam is an ax poised to cut him down and out of the academic life.

There is really no need, in most cases, for taking this attitude toward examinations. If one has cultivated good study habits, he should do well enough to have no fear of "flunking out," and he should approach an exam with an air of confidence and anticipation. The examination, after all, gives him a chance to show how much he knows and to receive his reward for the studying he has been doing. The examinations that come early in a course are opportunities to learn something about one's preparation and to correct any deficiencies in it. By profiting from them, the student is in a much better position to study effectively for the final examination and to do well on it. Instead of considering the instructor who gives many quizzes an ogre, the student should be grateful that the instructor is willing to spend so much of his time helping his students learn.

One of the nasty things about examinations is that students frequently "blow up" and get

so tense and unnerved that they do much less than their best. They forget things they knew just a little while before, make silly mistakes, and lose all sense of what is important and unimportant.

Probably the best medicine for this disease is to be prepared. If you go into an examination prepared as well as you can ever expect to be, you don't need to get upset. You'll do your best, and that's that!

This point has an important psychological sidelight. Many a student does not realize that "going to pieces" during an examination is frequently an alibi he has given himself. He blows up not only because he isn't prepared and knows he isn't prepared but also because he then doesn't need to feel guilty about not being prepared. "Test anxiety" is often a childish defense the student puts up against taking the blame for his own lack of preparation.

Besides being well prepared, there are a few other things you can do to quell your excitement or anxious feelings. One is to allow yourself plenty of time to do what you need to do before the exam and still get there a little ahead of the bell. Don't let yourself get in a rush; this merely aggravates your excitement and further disorganizes you. A second thing to do is to relax deliberately just before the examination and while you are waiting for it to be handed out. Don't try to do a last-minute review, skimming through your notes or your book. Don't get into arguments with other students about some fine point in your notes; this merely upsets you. Remember you can't do anything worthwhile in such a short time; all you can do by hectic, last-minute reviewing is confuse yourself with details and get yourself more excited. Rather, spend the few minutes just before an examination in small talk, reading the newspaper, or doing something that takes your mind off the "ordeal."

The last and most important thing you can do to keep yourself in hand is to have a plan of attack. It has been demonstrated over and over again in emergencies that people who know what to do and what they are going to do seldom get upset or panicky. The same applies to examinations. You probably know about what kind of examination to expect. There's a good sensible way to go about taking each kind. Know what it is, and be prepared to carry out your plan as soon as you get the signal to go ahead. We're going to describe these plans below. The important point, though, is that with a definite plan in mind you can keep calm and collected and thereby do yourself justice.

## TAKING OBJECTIVE EXAMINATIONS

Your plan in taking an objective examination is somewhat different from what it would be in taking an essay-type examination.

**Surveying.** When you pick up an objective test, first flip through the pages to see how many different kinds of question are being used: true-false, multiple-choice, matching, . . . ? See how many there are of each, and thus get an idea of how to divide your time during the examination. Usually, when the instructor uses more than one type of objective question, he segregates those of one type into one part, and this part is clearly labeled. By surveying the parts at the outset, you know what they are and thus what to expect.

**Knowing the ground rules.** Now begin taking the first part. It will have some directions. Read these carefully, and make sure you understand them. (You'd be surprised how many students don't.) Indicate your answers in exactly the way specified in the directions. If you don't, you may cause the instructor a lot of trouble and, more important, lose points merely because your answers aren't clear to the instructor.

Also when you tackle the questions in each part of the examination, make sure you understand the scoring rules, for these determine your strategy in taking the test. If there is no penalty for guessing, note that fact, and then proceed with the intention of answering every single question. Otherwise you are bound to

lose points by leaving some questions unanswered. If there is correction for chance, note that rule. In a true-false test, for example, you have a 50:50 chance of getting an answer correct simply by guessing. To correct for chance, an instructor may take a point off for a wrong answer and give only one point credit for a correct answer. (One formula for doing this is to score papers by taking the number right minus the number wrong.) This really isn't a penalty for guessing; it's merely a correction for chance. In such a case, your strategy should still be to guess and consequently to answer every question, for on the average your guesses will be more often right than wrong. On the other hand, if the scoring rule is to make a definite penalty for guessing, say, by taking two points off for a wrong answer while giving only one point credit for a correct one, then you must follow a conservative strategy. You should then answer only the questions of which you are reasonably sure.

The same principles apply to other types of objective examination. It is possible to score them so that there is no penalty for guessing or so that there is. The formula is usually too complicated to explain easily in an examination. Hence the instructor usually reduces it to a simple direction such as: "There is no penalty for guessing" or "Don't guess, for wrong answers will be penalized." Whatever the instruction, understand it and follow it carefully.

**Answering easy questions first.** Having gotten your instructions straight, you can proceed to read and answer questions. You must be prepared, however, to find some questions that are easy *for you* and others that are dif-

ficult. You must handle these questions differently. Those that are relatively easy you answer as soon as you've read them carefully and are sure of the answer. Those that you find more difficult and aren't certain about should be checked and passed by. Don't let them bog you down. If you struggle with them, you may waste precious time and later find yourself rushing through other questions, making mistakes on those you otherwise could get right. Instead, any time you are not certain you know the answer, put a check mark in the margin next to the question. After you've answered all the easy ones, you can come back to these. Knowing how much time you have left and how many tough ones there are, you can properly apportion the time available to spend on them.

The basic reason for this strategy is simple enough. In objective examinations, all the questions of the same kind usually count the same. You get no more credit for a difficult question than you do an easy one. You therefore don't want to become flustered by difficult ones or let them lower your score on the easy ones. We know from experience that this plan of taking objective questions can net a good many points; yet many students haven't learned it.

**Analyzing qualifiers.**  There is an art to reading and deciding on the correct answer to objective questions, and you can improve your examination results by learning it and practicing it. The following points should help you to do your best on objective questions:

True-false questions are usually constructed by taking two things or qualities and stating their relation to each other. The bare skeleton of the statement might be "Roses are red," "Attitudes are learned," or "The stock market crashed." Any such statement is usually true some of the time and not true at other times. You can't be expected to answer anything so ambiguous. The instructor never intended that you should. He is interested in knowing whether you know when and under what circumstances something is or is not true. So the statement usually is provided with qualifiers, and it's these qualifiers you should scrutinize carefully. Re-

member that in Chapter Four (page 36) we told you to retain essential qualifiers when you select main ideas and important details.

There are, of course, an infinite number of possible qualifiers, but a good many of them fall into one of the following series:

> *All, most, some, no*
> *Always, usually, sometimes, never*
> *Great, much, little, no*
> *More, equal, less*
> *Good, bad*
> *Is, is not*

If you run into a qualifier in one of these series or a qualifier that means essentially the same as one of these, your best way of testing whether the statement is true is to see whether you can substitute one of the other members in the series. If your substitution makes a statement that is better than the one you have, the question is false. If your substitution does not make a better statement, the question is true. Let's for example, take "Some roses are red." The alternative statements are "All roses are red," "Most roses are red," and "No roses are red." The two extreme statements are obviously less true. You may have doubts whether "Most roses are red" is true; but even if it is true, "Some roses are red" would also have to be true.

**Picking out key words.**  This way of analyzing qualifiers should be helpful in examinations even though real questions are naturally more complicated than these examples. It won't always work, but whether it does or not, it should help you find the *key* word or words in a statement. And there is always such a key. It may not be an adjective or adverb, but it will be a word or group of words on which the truth or falsity of the statement hinges. All the other words in the statement could form a statement that is either true or false depending on the key word(s). Look for this and don't worry about the possible exceptions to the other words in the statement.

Some students have picked up the idea that certain words automatically make a statement

## EXERCISE IN KEY WORDS

*The following quiz (from Clifford T. Morgan, Introduction to Psychology, McGraw-Hill, New York, 1943, p. 2), specifically designed both for students who have had a course in psychology and for those who have not, illustrates the importance of key words in objective questions. Take the quiz, picking out the key words and writing them in the space provided. In most cases, there is only one key word, but in a few instances, there are two or three. Also indicate in the right-hand column whether you think the statement is true or false. When you are finished, turn to page 76 for the correct answers.*

1. Geniuses are usually queerer than people of average intelligence.
2. Only human beings, not animals, have the capacity to think.
3. Much of human behavior is instinctive.
4. Slow learners remember what they learn better than fast learners.
5. Intelligent people form most of their opinions by logical reasoning.
6. A psychologist is a person who is trained to psychoanalyze people.
7. You can size up a person very well in an interview.
8. When one is working for several hours, it is better to take a few long rests than several short ones.
9. The study of mathematics exercises the mind so that a person can think more logically in other subjects.
10. Grades in college have little to do with success in business careers.
11. Alcohol, taken in small amounts, is a stimulant.
12. There is a clear distinction between the normal person and one who is mentally ill.
13. Prejudices are mainly due to lack of information.
14. Competition among people is characteristic of most human societies.
15. The feature of a job that is most important to employees is the pay they get for their work.
16. It is possible to classify people very well into introverts and extroverts.
17. Punishment is usually the best way of eliminating undesirable behavior in children.
18. By watching closely a person's expression, you can tell quite well the emotion he is experiencing.
19. The higher one sets his goals in life, the more he is sure to accomplish and the happier he will be.
20. If a person is honest with you, he usually can tell you what his motives are.

true or false. They know that it is difficult to construct true statements with such words as "no," "never," "every," or other sweeping qualifiers. They therefore mark such statements false whenever they occur. This is a dangerous practice, however, for instructors are just as aware of any giveaways as students are—usually more so. Consequently, they usually steer clear of statements that can be answered correctly by taking a cue from these simple extreme modifiers. On the other hand, they can sometimes construct statements containing these words that are, in fact, true. In some cases, especially in the natural sciences, blunt unqualified statements are true. Such statements will catch (and they properly should) the student who isn't judging them on their merits.

The best true-false questions usually are one-clause statements, but occasionally they may be constructed in two clauses. Then they are really two statements, not one. If you encounter such a question, judge each of the two statements separately. If one of them is false, even if the other seems true, mark the question false. Usually, though, both statements are either true or false.

**Reading multiple-choice questions.**    Multiple-choice questions are basically true-false questions arranged in groups. A lead phrase or clause at the beginning of the question combines with three or more endings to make different statements. Sometimes the questions are so constructed that any number of the statements in a question can be true or false. Then the question is really several true-false statements, and all that we have said above applies. Make sure, however, to read directions care-fully so that you can answer the questions as they are supposed to be answered.

Most typically, the multiple-choice question differs from the true-false item in that only one alternative out of the group is to be selected. Hence your job is to pick the alternative that is *more nearly true* than the others. It's a relative matter, not one of absolute truth or falsity. This fact dictates certain tactics in dealing with the question.

Read carefully through the question once and spot those alternatives that are clearly false. To help dispose of them, you can cross out the letter or number that precedes these false statements. Now concentrate on those that may be true. Read them again, note and test the key words as you would in a true-false statement, and compare the items to see which seems to be the more nearly true. Once you've made a decision, mark the answer in the appropriate space and go on to the next question. If you can't make up your mind, place a check mark at the side of the question and leave it until you can come back later to work on the more difficult questions.

**Reading other types of question.**    Similar methods are applicable to *matching questions*. Read down all the items to be matched in one question in order to get an idea of the range of possibilities you're up against. Then take the first item on the left and read down the items on the right until you find one you're sure is the best match. If you're not certain, leave the item and go on to the next one. The general idea is to fill in first all the matches you are sure of. That then reduces the number of possibilities for the difficult matches and simpli-

## ANSWERS FOR EXERCISE IN KEY WORDS

*The key words for each question were as follows: (1) usually, (2) only, not, (3) much, (4) better, (5) most, (6) psychoanalyze, (7) very well, (8) better, (9) in other subjects, (10) little, (11) stimulant, (12) clear, (13) mainly, (14) most, (15) most important, (16) very well, (17) usually, best, (18) quite well, (19) sure, happier, (20) usually. All the statements are false. The reasons for their being false can be found in the book from which they were taken or, very likely, in any general course in psychology.*

fies the job. Some matching questions consist only of words or brief phrases to be matched up. Others may contain whole clauses similar to those in true-false or multiple-choice statements. In this latter case, try to spot key words and test them as we have suggested above for true-false and multiple-choice questions.

One type of question used fairly commonly in large courses is the *completion question*. This provides a statement much like a true-false statement except that one word or a phrase is left out and you must supply it. When you answer such questions, choose your words carefully, for the instructor has something pretty specific in mind: a technical term or a key word in some main idea or important detail. Try to find the answer that really belongs. On the other hand, if you cannot think of the answer that is called for, write down something that represents your best guess. Often such answers, even though they're not exactly what is wanted, get complete or partial credit.

**The course is the context.**   One general bit of advice about objective tests seems in order because we've had so many occasions to tell it to students in examination situations: Always remember that the context of the questions is the course you're taking. In answering a question, ask yourself how this question should be answered in the light of your textbook or what has been said in class. If possible, identify its source, from textbook or class. If you can't do that, search your memory for anything you've learned in the course that's relevant. Don't answer the question according to the latest magazine you've read, your personal opinion, or some other course you've taken. Sometimes that would give you a different answer, for all answers are relative to a given context and source of information. The instructor, in framing his questions, cannot be responsible for your personal reading habits, but he can reasonably expect you to answer in terms of the course he is giving you.

**Finishing up the examination.**   We've said that you should read through an objective ex-

amination, answering the easy questions and coming back later to the hard ones. When you start to work on the hard ones, see how much time you have left and allocate it among the questions you still must do. However, in planning this time, leave some for a final rereading of your examination. Before you turn in your examination, you should read it through again carefully just in case you have made any foolish mistakes, like putting down a different answer than you intended or leaving some questions unanswered.

When you reread your examination, you'll probably be tempted to change some of your answers. We have some sound advice on this point. If you feel strongly that an answer should be changed, change it. On the other hand, if you waver between two answers, not being able to make up your mind, don't change the answer you set down originally. A lot of research on this point has shown that, when you are guessing, your first guess, based on a careful reading, is likely to be your best guess. If you change your answers when you're quite unsure of yourself, the chances are that you're doing the wrong thing. Remember, your first guess is probably your best.

## TAKING ESSAY EXAMINATIONS

We'll use the term "essay" to refer to any examination in which the questions themselves are relatively brief and most of your work is in composing answers to these questions. Essay examinations may consist, at one extreme, of "short-answer" questions, which require you to write down a rather specific list of things. At the other extreme are "discussion" questions, which ask you to cover a rather broad subject at some length. In Chapter Nine we'll consider examinations that involve working out problems.

**Planning your time.**   In taking essay examinations, even more than objective tests, you must plan and allocate your time. Even if you're not an outstanding student, you have sufficient knowledge to write much more than you have time for and you may get carried away on certain questions you know the most about. Hence, if you're not careful, you can spend far too much time on some questions and end up giving others short shrift. If you do this, you'll usually draw a low grade on some questions, for the instructor rightly expects you to budget your time and give each question its proportionate share.

To strike such a balance in your examination, read the whole examination through before you start to write anything. See how much time you are expected to spend on each question. If this isn't stated, make an estimate of the time you think should be spent on each, and try to stick to it as you work.

If the examination offers you options permitting you to take some questions and omit others, make a tentative decision at the outset. Choose and mark the questions you're sure you can write on. If you're in doubt about any, let

these go until you can think about them a little and make a decision. Be sure to number correctly each question you answer.

**Following directions.** Essay questions, like objective ones, have key words. But in this case, the key words are really instructions to you for writing on the question. The key words are usually those such as "list," "illustrate," "compare," and "outline." Each means something different from the other, and the instructor chose the one he wanted for a good reason. Students are tempted to "write around" a subject and to tell what they know about it whether they were asked to or not. They do this especially if they aren't prepared to do exactly what the key word calls for. This, however, is a waste of time, for the instructor usually ignores what he doesn't ask for and considers the student to be evading the question that was put to him. You should therefore note the key

## IMPORTANT WORDS IN ESSAY QUESTIONS

*The following terms appear frequently in the phrasing of essay questions. You should know their meaning and answer accordingly. (The list and the sense of the definitions, though not the exact words, are adapted from C. Bird*

**Compare**

Look for qualities or characteristics that resemble each other. Emphasize similarities among them, but in some cases also mention differences.

**Contrast**

Stress the dissimilarities, differences, or unlikenesses of things, qualities, events, or problems.

**Criticize**

Express your judgment about the merit or truth of the factors or views mentioned. Give the results of your analysis of these factors, discussing their limitations and good points.

**Define**

Give concise, clear, and authoritative meanings. Don't give details, but make sure to give the limits of the definition. Show how the thing you are defining differs from things in other classes.

**Describe**

Recount, characterize, sketch, or relate in sequence or story form.

**Diagram**

Give a drawing, chart, plan, or graphic answer. Usually you should label a diagram. In some cases, add a brief explanation or description.

**Discuss**

Examine, analyze carefully, and give reasons pro and con. Be complete, and give details.

**Enumerate**

Write in list or outline form, giving points concisely one by one.

**Evaluate**

Carefully appraise the problem, citing both advantages and limitations. Emphasize the appraisal of authorities and, to a lesser degree, your personal evaluation.

**Explain**

Clarify, interpret, and spell out the material you present. Give reasons for differences of opinion or of results, and try to analyze causes.

word in the question and then stick as closely as possible to what it implies. If it is "list," don't discuss or illustrate, except possibly as a way of adding pertinent information to your list; if it says, "illustrate," illustrate; don't list, discuss, or compare; and so on.

**Outlining.** When you're sure you understand what is called for in a question, it is best to outline in your mind the main points you're going to use in answering the question. You can jot this outline down by putting key words in the upper right-hand part of the page. Then use this outline as a guide in writing your answer. After you're through with it, you can cross it out so that it won't be mistaken as part of your answer. The grader won't mind, for he expects good students to do exactly this. If you don't outline, you're likely to "free-associate" and get off the track somewhere. You may, in your rush, forget one or two of the important points. By making an outline first, you can write a much more coherent, succinct, and complete answer.

It is a good idea, too, to write your answer in some kind of outline. It shouldn't be too skimpy or consist of incomplete sentences because the grader then won't know what you mean. You can indicate your outline, however, by using numbers for your main points and possibly letters for subordinate points and by indenting. Part of the purpose of an essay question is to test your ability to organize, and this is one way of showing clearly what your organization is. Moreover, the grader who grades a lot of papers gets a little weary trudging through endless paragraphs of answers. He looks for any cues that make easier his job of telling what you know. You're much more likely to get credit for your knowledge if you express it in well-organized outline form than if you just ramble along.

*and D. M. Bird,* Learning More by Effective Study, *Appleton-Century-Crofts, New York, 1945, pp. 195–198.*)

**Illustrate**

Use a figure, picture, diagram, or concrete example to explain or clarify a problem.

**Interpret**

Translate, give examples of, solve, or comment on, a subject, usually giving your judgment about it.

**Justify**

Prove or give reasons for decisions or conclusions, taking pains to be convincing.

**List**

As in "enumerate," write an itemized series of concise statements.

**Outline**

Organize a description under main points and subordinate points, omitting minor details and stressing the arrangement or classification of things.

**Prove**

Establish that something is true by citing factual evidence or giving clear logical reasons.

**Relate**

Show how things are related to, or connected with, each other or how one causes another, correlates with another, or is like another.

**Review**

Examine a subject critically, analyzing and commenting on the important statements to be made about it.

**State**

Present the main points in brief, clear sequence, usually omitting details, illustrations, or examples.

**Summarize**

Give the main points or facts in condensed form, like the summary of a chapter, omitting details and illustrations.

**Trace**

In narrative form describe progress, development, or historical events from some point of origin.

**Being explicit.** Students commonly make the mistake of expressing their points in brief, sketchy language and then expecting the grader to know exactly what was intended. They often choose their words carelessly, and the grader, not being a mind reader, isn't sure whether the student actually knows what he is talking about or is just bluffing. For that reason, it is important to nail down every point you make. Say it as precisely as you can the first time, but then give an illustration or an important relevant detail or something that makes it clear that you know what you're talking about. Thus you can convince the grader, whereas otherwise you won't be credited for something you may really know.

Elaborating your point in this way, however, is not the same thing as "padding." Students often bring in extraneous points or say the same thing in slightly different ways just to bulk their otherwise slim answers. Most graders, having read hundreds of papers, can spot this sort of thing quickly, and they don't have a kindly attitude toward it. It's better to be

## ORGANIZING ESSAY ANSWERS

*Here are two examples of brief answers to an essay question. Read them to see what you think of them, and then compare your judgment with our comment at the end. The question is: What were the important results of the (English) revolution of 1688?*

### The first answer

I will summarize the most important results of the revolution under three headings:

1. *Parliament's victory.* The most direct result of the revolution of 1688 was the final victory of Parliament in the conflict between it and the crown that had gone on all during the 17th century. Parliament, by declaring the throne vacant because of James II's desertion to France, finally established that the king ruled by choice of the people and Parliament and not by divine right. Parliament established a Bill of Rights, which said that the king was not above the law but was himself subject to the law. In the early years of the reign of William and Mary, many additional acts were passed which curtailed the powers of the crown.

2. *The end of religious conflict.* The revolution itself did not entirely end the religious troubles of the 17th century, but Parliament passed a Toleration Act which brought an end to many of the difficulties of the Dissenters. The Catholics, however, were still subjected to many infringements of civil liberties.

3. *A new political class.* The important general result

of the revolution and the victory of Parliament was the beginning of a long era during which political power in England was divided between the landed gentry and the merchant class.

### The second answer

The revolution of 1688 was very important. It was so important that it is sometimes called the "glorious revolution." Parliament won, and it passed a lot of acts which were against the king, and it invited William and Mary to rule jointly in England. William and Mary still had to fight though, especially in Ireland where James II was finally defeated. William and Mary cooperated with Parliament so there wasn't so much trouble between the King and Parliament. James II was very unpopular because he was a Catholic, and Parliament made it so no Catholic could ever become king again, although Parliament made things easier for the Dissenters. This was the end of the Divine Right of kings in England, though at first the country was ruled mostly by the aristocracy and the rich merchants. Real democracy didn't come until much later, so the revolution of 1688 wasn't a completely democratic revolution.

*Notice that these two answers differ more in organization than they do in content. The first answer is not perfect, but it is balanced, clear, and factual. The second is much the poorer because it is vague, disorganized, and full of irrelevancies and loose statements.*

brief than to pad with irrelevancies. That way you don't reveal your ignorance or seem to be bluffing.

**Handwriting and good English.** Far too many students have atrocious handwriting. Some student hands are almost impossible to read, and others can be read only with difficulty. If you have one of these, try to do something about it. You may never write a clear, beautiful hand, but you can at least be legible. And it is important that you do, for instructors feel that a student should be able to write legibly; they can't give him credit for something they can't read. Some instructors will try hard to decipher illegible writing, but others have no patience at all with it and summarily mark down the illegible or poorly legible paper. In one research, for example, a group of graders twice graded the same papers, once when the papers were difficult to read and at another time when they were written in a clear hand. The graders' instructions were to pay no attention to handwriting in arriving at their grades. Nevertheless, the grades assigned to the legible papers were a full grade higher than those given to the hardly legible papers, though the two sets contained exactly the same answers. If your writing is hard to read, remember that it may make the difference between a C and a D or an A and a B. That's a lot. If your writing is hard to decipher, you'd better start practicing better handwriting.

You should also take pains to write good English, that is, to use good grammar, punctuate properly, and spell correctly. Aside from making a good impression, all are necessary for easy reading and even to understanding what you are trying to say. To the grader, poor grammar implies disorganized, confused thinking and inadequate command of the subject mat-ter. Poor spelling, especially of important words, reflects not only careless reading and study but inadequate knowledge and understanding of the material. Hence it is only natural that mistakes of this sort will pull your grade down whether the grader intends them to or not. So in your hurry to write an answer, don't forget to observe the elementary rules of good English.

**Learning from examinations.** We'll wind up this chapter on taking examinations by pointing out that you can learn a great deal from them. When the typical student gets his paper back, he looks to see whether the instructor made any error in marking his paper and whether there is anything to quibble about. Then he puts the paper aside and does nothing more with it. Sometimes errors in grading do occur, and a student should point them out to the instructor. More important, however, by studying his paper carefully, the student can learn a lot about his past preparation and his ways of preparing for the next examination.

Where you've made mistakes or lost credit, look the matter up in your notes or in the book to see exactly how this came about. Did you misinterpret something in the course? Did you fail to get something important into your notes and study it? Did you fail to note the important qualifiers? Did you misread the question? These and other queries can be answered by studying your examination paper. In this way, you may uncover characteristic faults in your study habits and then proceed to correct them. All of us probably learn more by correcting our mistakes than we do from our successes, and an examination paper is a concrete record of mistakes. You'll be wise to profit from them.

SEVEN

WRITING

THEMES

AND REPORTS

Previous chapters cover pretty well the general problems of college study. But you will run into some specific matters that we haven't dealt with yet. In the next few chapters, we'll try to give you guidance in handling some particular problems that are likely to come your way. We begin in this chapter with the writing of themes and reports.

Most freshmen are required to take a course in English composition. Its purpose is to help you learn to write accurately and understandably; if you give it half a chance, it generally will. Usually, in a course of this sort, you write a number of themes or compositions, and the instructor corrects these, not so much for the purpose of giving you a grade as to point out to you what things you are doing wrong.

For many students, this business of writing themes is an odious and frustrating task. For some who don't do well in it, it spells doom to their college career. Those who merely get through the course move on to their upper classes only to find that they have more themes and papers to write. Finding the task unpleasant, they put off writing the paper until the end of the term and then do it hastily and inadequately, with disappointing consequences for them and their instructors.

Such discomfort and failure don't have to be. Few of you will become professional writers, but just about all of you who graduate from college will find that your jobs and positions in the community require you to write well enough to be able to communicate something to other people. Even a sales report is better if it is well written. In short, you can and should learn to write well if you are going to make the most of your college education.

In this chapter we will try to provide some help for writing term papers and themes. We won't say everything that could be said about writing because most of you will sometime take a course in English composition, and there are also a good many handbooks of composition and manuals on writing that can help you.

## GRAMMAR AND WRITING

The main purpose of writing is to tell people something, to communicate. The basic difference between good writing and bad writing lies in how well it tells you what the writer had in his mind. Of course, some writing is literature, and literature has an aesthetic as well as an informative purpose. Very few of you will be much concerned about literary writing, however; your main job is to learn how to write clearly and effectively.

That's where grammar comes in. Sometimes students get the idea that grammar was invented for the sole purpose of tripping them up and making life hard for them. And in the case of some picayune points of grammar, this idea is not very far from wrong. The rules of grammar you are likely to learn in a good modern course in English composition, however, are realistic and practical. Their main purpose is to help you to write and speak effectively and to understand something about the language you have used all your life.

Good writing is built on good grammar. And the rules of good grammar come from good writing. It's that simple! If something is clear, easy to understand, and not clumsy, it is grammatically correct. "Aha," you may say, "a statement like 'He sure ain't a real friendly dog' is clear and easy to understand, but it has several mistakes in grammar." As a matter of fact, such a statement is good grammar—good colloquial grammar. It is the kind of thing many people would say, and other people would understand them.

The important point, however, is that spoken language often doesn't look right in print because it is inappropriate to a diverse audience. Good grammatical writing is appropriate to the occasion. In written English people usually don't expect a word like "ain't" or an adjective like "sure" modifying a verb. Written English is more formal than spoken English mostly because formal writing is more exact and precise than informal writing. So when you write a theme or an essay, you try to be a little more formal. That's all. You don't try to be complicated or try to remember confusing and obscure rules of grammar. You learn a few simple rules, and you apply these in a sensible way. Above all, you continually ask yourself, "Is what I am writing clear, and does it say what I really mean?"

**Punctuation.**　Punctuation is the backbone of good writing, and we can use it to show you how sensible good grammar can be. The surprising thing is that anybody can punctuate properly just by doing a little thinking. The purpose of periods and commas is to set apart separate ideas so that you can digest them without being confused by other ideas.

The period is the basic punctuation mark, and you use it any time you have an idea that is complete. For example, you can have a one-word sentence: "Stop." Here is a whole idea expressed by one word.

When do you know that you have a complete idea? For one thing, just talking out loud will help. Your intonation changes at the end of a sentence, and you pause. The change in intonation and the pause are a way of putting periods into what you say out loud. Thus you can just put periods where your intonation falls and you pause. This won't always work, but it makes the important point that punctuation in writing is just as easy as punctuation in talking. You punctuate in talking all the time without thinking about it. The trouble with many people is that they do not have enough experience at punctuating in writing, and they are not sure of themselves.

Commas are used to separate ideas that are related. If one idea depends upon another, they should be separated by a comma (just as the ideas in this sentence are). Commas also separate out words for emphasis or in enumeration (when you are listing things), again in much the same way that you use emphasis and pauses in speaking.

Of course, many people are very fussy about the formal rules of punctuation, many of which are merely traditional. If you really have trouble with punctuating or if you're going to do some writing aimed at people who are very particular about the proper way to write, you had better find a handbook of composition or grammar and look into the rules for punctuating. Don't lose sight, though, of the purpose of punctuation. Punctuation is there to keep ideas apart and in this way to make things easy to read and understand. Sometimes it is very nice (and useful) to use elegant variations in punctuation. But if you tackle some of the more complicated rules, always keep the basic purpose of punctuation in mind.

**The use of mistakes.** Everybody makes mistakes in grammar. This is just another way of saying that the writing of most of us can stand some improvement. Some people make mistakes in rather elementary matters, however, and these are usually the people who run into trouble in writing themes and essays. If you ignore the really basic rules of grammar, you make your writing hard to read and leave the impression that you're ignorant and really not very bright. Frequently, however, students ignore basic rules because they are not in the

## DICTIONARIES CAN HELP WITH PUNCTUATION

*Here is part of a page of the section on punctuation in a dictionary. (By permission. From* Webster's New Collegiate Dictionary, *copyright 1949, 1951, 1953, 1956, by G. & C. Merriam Company.)*

# PUNCTUATION

### The chief marks of punctuation and reference, with their names.

| | | |
|---|---|---|
| , Comma. | ` (è)  Grave accent. | / Virgule. |
| ; Semicolon. | ∧ *or* ^ *or* ~  Circumflex. | { *or* }  Brace. |
| : Colon. | ˜ (ñ)  Tilde. | * * * *or* ——  Ellipsis. |
| . Period, *or* full stop. | – (ō)  Macron. | . . .  Ellipsis; *also*, leaders. |
| — Dash. | ˘ (ŏ)  Breve. | * Asterisk. |
| ? Interrogation point. | ¨ (oö)  Diaeresis. | † Dagger. |
| ! Exclamation point. | ˛ (ç)  Cedilla. | ‡ Double dagger. |
| ( ) Parentheses, *or* curves. | ∧ Caret. | § Section; *also*, numbered clause. |
| [ ] Brackets. | " " *also* " "  Quotation marks. | ‖ Parallels. |
| ' Apostrophe. | « »  Quotation marks, French. | ¶ *or* ℙ  Paragraph. |
| - Hyphen. | » « *or* „ "  Quotation marks, German. | ☞ Index, *or* fist. |
| ´ (é)  Acute accent. | ' ' *also* ' '  Quotation marks, single. | * * *or* *\** Asterism. |

The chief uses of the most important punctuation marks are explained in the numbered sections below. These directions represent preferred American usage; permissible alternatives and British differences are sometimes but not always shown below. The directions represent usage in continuous textual matter; these practices may be varied for special purposes in display printing, in tabulated matter, or in certain condensed styles of compilation.

### 1. THE PERIOD, OR FULL STOP [.]

A period is used at the end of a sentence, or any expression standing for a sentence, that is neither interrogative nor exclamatory.

Society is a wave.  The wave moves onward, but the water of which it is composed does not.  The same particle does not rise from the valley to the ridge.
Please close the door.  Certainly.

**A period is used after an abbreviation.**

Reedville, Montg. Co., pop. 879; cap. or l. c.; n. masc.; 7 a.m.; 30 mins.; lg. pkg.; no. 72; 5s. 6d.; 50 m.p.h.; bks. marked o.p. [or op]; dept. bulls.; *Tech. Bull.*, mo., 50 pp.; U.S.S. *Wyoming;* Dr. and Mrs. Jas. Brown, 7 Pine St., Bath, Ohio; David Livingstone, LL.D. (b. 1813, d. 1873); raid of Apr. 18, 1942 led by Lt. Col. James H. Doolittle.

Exceptions.  Abbreviations of compound names of international organizations and government agencies, official abbreviations designating equipment, and a large number of similar compound abbreviations are preferably written without periods and without spaces:

ABCD powers; ILO; UNRRA; UN; USSR; MVD; MGB; SEC; TVA; Pfc; GI; PX; PT; TD; VT fuze; IOU; ESP; IPA; MS.

NOTE 1.  Many common contractions (with omission of medial letters) are preferably written as abbreviations with periods:

secy. (preferred to sec'y); advt.; mfg.; recd.; Dr. (debtor).

An ellipsis or a suspension may be indicated by a row of spaced periods, commonly three periods (in the use of some authorities four periods) in addition to punctuation marks required at the beginning and end of the ellipsis; thus, four periods (or five) are used when the omitted words constitute a whole sentence or the last words of a sentence or when the omission falls at the end of the quotation and at the same time at the end of the main sentence.

As ellipsis marks these periods are used to indicate intentional omission of one or more words or sentences from quoted matter as nonessential to the present purpose, also to indicate illegible or unquotable words, dashes being commoner for this last purpose.

"Now that wars . . . have become far more horrible and . . . insane."
*Dean Inge.*
"A good deal . . . hangs on the meaning . . . of this short word."
*T. S. Eliot.*
We quote from Keats's *Endymion:*
  Now with aught else can our souls interknit
  So wingedly . . . . [not the end of sentence in Keats]
Belial's well-known lines:
  Sad cure! for who would lose
  Though full of pain, this intellectual being. . . ?
*Paradise Lost* II. 146

habit of carefully examining what they write. Take, for example, the matter of agreement between subject and verb.

Nearly all of you can recognize that "He don't care" is not good written English. (And most of you can put your finger on exactly what is wrong. If you can't, you probably have some very serious trouble with your writing and you ought to see someone who can help you.) The correct form is "He does not [doesn't] care," and it is correct because a singular subject belongs with one form of the verb ("does") and not another ("do").

Many students fail to make the subject and verb agree not because they are ignorant but because they are too careless to read carefully what they have written. Many students would write "A group of people were standing on the corner" because, without thinking, they would make the verb "were" agree with the noun "people." But the subject of this sentence is "group," not "people." "Group" is a singular noun (like "everybody" and "mob"), and it takes a singular verb ("was").

Little mistakes like this are not terribly important by themselves, but teachers of composition are concerned about them because students who make them are usually students who do not understand the English language as well as they ought to. Can you, for example, always identify the subject of a sentence? Or do you confuse the subject with any noun or with some part of the sentence that merely modifies the subject?

The real purpose of studying grammar is not to avoid trivial mistakes but to help you avoid writing things that are so unclear that they do not mean anything to anyone but you. Knowing something about grammar isn't the only thing that is important in good writing, but it is one of the things that is most important.

That is the reason for the title of this section. We really didn't intend to give you a list of the "ten most common mistakes in grammar," but we mean to show you that you can make use of your mistakes and, by correcting them, improve your writing.

When someone corrects a mistake, always make sure you know what the correct form is and, even more important, make sure that you know why you made the mistake. This is the only good way you learn the proper use of your language. Get into the habit of carefully reading what you write in order to correct your own little mistakes. You will find that this is actually interesting. But, above all, if you don't understand why you made a mistake or why a correction was made, find out. If you don't, you will be handicapped all through college.

Give up the notion that grammar is a capricious set of rules made up just to trouble

## HOW'S YOUR GRAMMAR?

*To assess a person's grammar and ability to punctuate requires a fairly lengthy and detailed test. You may take such a test when you enter college or take a course in English writing. If, however, you are unusually poor in grammar and punctuation, you will miss some of the items on the following brief test. See page 86 for the correct answers after you have taken the test. Underline the correct alternative.*

1. Either history or economics (is, are) going to be my major.
2. The size of clothes (is, are) much too small for him.
3. Everybody wants to do (his, their) best.
4. The fellow asked me (who, whom) my teacher was.
5. She, like Jane and (I, me), is pretty tall.
6. Each of us (look, looks) forward to seeing her.
7. We have (began, begun) the college team.
8. He had (lain, laid) there for some time.
9. He called me "(The, the) smartest fellow of them all."
10. The title of the article was "(The, the) (Cool, cool) of the (Night, night)."

you. The rules of grammar actually come from the way you and other people write and talk. Knowing them helps you to write and talk in the way other people do and to understand what they are saying. If you had your own unique way of writing and talking, that would be fine, except that nobody could understand you. Only by making your writing and speech conform to other people's can you make it possible for other people to understand you.

**Spelling.**    A brief but emphatic word about spelling: As a college student, you're expected to spell correctly *all* the words you write. That includes not only the common words everybody uses but also the rarer and more technical words (and names) encountered in college training. To spell correctly all the time, you must do the following things: First of all, be careful. Students often misspell words they know how to spell simply because they're careless; they write hurriedly and don't look for their own spelling errors. Secondly, pay attention to the spelling of the new words and names you come across in studying. Make sure you can spell any of the names or important words in your textbooks or in the sources you use for writing papers. Thirdly, use the dictionary. Any time you are in the slightest doubt about spelling, look up the word in the dictionary. Finally, familiarize yourself with spelling rules, particularly for the special endings of words. You can find these rules in grammar books and also in dictionaries.

Misspelled words are serious offenses. They distract a reader's attention because they look odd, making him stop to see what's wrong when he should be concerned only with the meaning of what he reads. Spelling is also taken as a mark of the cultural training of an individual; if you don't spell well, you give the impression of being illiterate and poorly educated. Finally, a teacher takes the misspelling of special words and names as a sign that the student hasn't really mastered the material he is writing about. One student we know got an F on an otherwise good paper on Shakespeare's *Julius Caesar* because he repeatedly wrote Mark Anthony for the correct Mark Antony. Not every teacher would assess such a heavy penalty—though the error was "inexcusable"—but all are displeased and unfavorably impressed by misspelled words. A student who hopes to do well on his papers had therefore better be a good speller.

## AIDS TO WRITING

Teachers and other people can show you how to make your speech and writing better, but in the long run, straightening out your grammar is something only you can do. Like most skills, grammatical skill comes only through practice. If you worry about your writing only when you have to write a theme or term paper, you won't improve much. To acquire grammatical skill, you must make your use of language a continuing project for improvement.

We can make a few suggestions that will help you in this project: First of all, you must have and use a good dictionary. There are several excellent dictionaries, and perhaps you have had one or more of them recommended to you by your instructor in English writing. If not, you might investigate those available in your college bookstore. Any dictionary comparable in size and quality to the *Webster's New Collegiate Dictionary* will do.

Just having a dictionary isn't enough, though. Get into the habit of consulting it every chance you get. You'll be surprised at the amount of information you'll find in it. First of all, of course, dictionaries can tell you how to spell words, and most of us find it necessary to use

## KEY FOR HOW'S YOUR GRAMMAR?

*The following are the correct answers: (1) is, (2) is, (3) his, (4) who, (5) me, (6) looks, (7) begun, (8) lain, (9) the, (10) The, Cool, Night.*

# A PAGE FROM A DICTIONARY OF USAGE

*From H. W. Fowler,* A Dictionary of Modern English Usage, *Oxford, New York, 1944. By permission of the publishers.*

**VICE-QUEEN**      693      **VIEW**

for *vicegerent*, & sometimes used pleonastically for *regent* (which word includes the notion of vice-), so that it seems to have no right to exist, & may be classed among SUPERFLUOUS WORDS.

**vice-queen)(vicereine.** The first is recorded from the 16th c., the second (in English) from the 19th only. *Vicereine* is now the regular word for viceroy's wife, & *vice-queen*, in much less frequent use, is now reserved for a woman ruling as a queen's representative—a useful DIFFERENTIATION.

**viceregal)(viceroyal.** There being no distinction of meaning, it would be better if there were one word only ; *viceregal* is the better, & *viceroyal* may fairly be called a SUPERFLUOUS WORD.

**vicinage** is now, compared with *neighbourhood*, a FORMAL WORD, &, compared with *vicinity*, a dying one.

**vicious circle.** See under TECHNICAL TERMS. *There is a vicious circle in which starvation produces Bolshevism, & Bolshevism in its turn* feeds on *starvation*. What, then, produces starvation, & on what does starvation feed ? The writer can no doubt retort with truth that nothing (i.e. no food) produces starvation, & that starvation feeds on nothing ; but he will have proved his wit at the expense of his logic. Such blunders in stating the elements of a vicious circle are not uncommon.

**victimize** makes *-zable* ; see MUTE E.
**victress.** FEMININE DESIGNATIONS.
**victual.** The verb makes *-ller*, *-lling*, see -LL-, -L- ; pronounce vĭ'tl, vĭ'tler, vĭ'tlĭng.

**vide.** Pronounce vī'dĭ ; literally ' see ' (imperative). It is properly used in referring readers to a passage in which they will find a proof or illustration of what has been stated, & should be followed by something in the nature of chapter & verse, or at least by the name of a book or author. But it has, like RE, been taken over by the illiterate, & is daily used by them in extended senses with an incongruity of which the following is a comparatively mild specimen : *Numbers count for nothing—vide the Coalition—it is the principles that tell.*

**videlicet** in its full form is now rare except in PEDANTIC HUMOUR, the abbreviation *viz* being used instead ; see VIZ for meaning.

**vidimus.** Pl. *-uses* ; see -US. Pronounce vĭ'dĭ-.
**vie.** For inflexions, see VERBS IN -IE &c., 3.
**view** forms part of three well established idioms each equivalent to a preposition, & each liable to be confused in meaning or in form with the others. These are *in v. of*, *with a v. to*, & *with the v. of*. *In view of* means taking into account, or not forgetting, or considering, & is followed by a noun expressing external circumstances that exist or must be expected : *In v. of these facts, we have no alternative* ; *In v. of his having promised amendment* ; *In v. of the Judgement to come.* With *a view to* means calculating upon or contemplating as a desired result, & is followed by a verbal noun or a gerund or less idiomatically an infinitive : *With a v. to diminution of waste*, or *to diminishing waste*, or (less well) *to diminish waste.* With *the view of* has the same meaning as *with a v. to*, but is both less usual & less flexible, being naturally followed only by a gerund : *With the v. of proving his sanity.* It will be observed that in the first phrase *v.* means sight, in the second eye, & in the third purpose. The forms of confusion are giving the first the meaning of the others or vice versa, & neglecting the correspondences *a* & *to*, *the* & *of*, in the second & third. After each of the following quotations a correction, or a statement that it is right, is bracketed :— *There was very little likelihood in the report of disaster to a Turkish destroyer in harbour at Preveza,* in view of *the fact that no Turkish destroyer was stationed there* (right)./

a dictionary for this purpose fairly often. Secondly, dictionaries can tell you the meanings of words and how to use them. One of the best things you can do to improve your study habits is to become a definition hunter. Whenever you find a word that puzzles you or a strange use of a familiar word, look it up in the dictionary. You'll find that such regular use of a dictionary helps a lot to lighten the load of reading an obscure or difficult textbook.

You'll also find a lot of useful miscellaneous information in the dictionary. It usually contains a terse but adequate summary of grammar. In many dictionaries there is a gazetteer (look that word up in the dictionary—you will probably be surprised) and a list of the names and principal works of famous people. These things are all useful.

Besides a dictionary, it is a good idea to have handy a good book on grammar. Your textbook for English composition will probably do for this purpose; but if you want to buy something special, the *Century Collegiate Handbook* is worth the money. This contains not only sensible rules about the use of English but also lots of examples of correct and incorrect usage.

If you are really going to do quite a little writing or feel that you would really like to master the use of your language, a copy of Fowler's *A Dictionary of Modern English Usage* or its American counterpart, *A Dictionary of American-English Usage,* is indispensable. Finally, to fill out your collection, you might add Roget's *Thesaurus . . .* , which

classifies and relates English words and phrases. These are books you'll find on the desk of nearly everyone who does a lot of writing, from editors of machine-tool trade magazines to literary critics.

## USING THE LIBRARY

When you write a theme or short composition, you may not need very much in the way of articles or books you don't already have at hand. What you can recall from personal experience may be enough. Term papers, however, are usually different. They require you to do some research, to learn something that you didn't know before. Indeed, that is one of the real values of doing term papers.

The library is the place you must go to gather your materials. Everybody uses the library once in a while; but if you've never written a term paper before, you may not know all the things that even a small library can do for you. If you've done no more than go to the library to study, to take out a book, or to hunt down assigned reading, you really don't know how to use the library. Hence we should tell you about some of the things you will find in the library that are absolutely essential for writing good term papers.

The backbone of any college library is its reference books. These are apt to be forbidding-looking volumes with titles like *United States Statistical Abstracts.* Learning how to use these books is an essential part of a college education, and it may be one of the parts you will be most thankful for later on.

These reference books are the places to look for information about topics so bewildering that you hardly know where to begin. If you already know what specific articles or books you want to read in order to write a particular paper, you won't have too much occasion to use the reference books. Lots of times, however, you are going to be so much at sea that these reference books will be your only hope. In this section we're going to describe some of them and tell you what they are used for and how to use them.

**Statistical sources.** If you are after statistical information about matters of general interest, the first place to look is in one of the common collections of statistical information. *The World Almanac* and the *Information Please Almanac* are two such books. You have probably heard about these at one time or another, but perhaps you really haven't noticed how much you can find in them. As a matter of fact, they are so useful and so inexpensive that it is really worth your while buying one of them. If you don't own one, however, you will find them in the library. There is hardly a subject, from weather and geography to baseball and music, that isn't in one or both of them. They both have very good indexes, and if you want to know something about pig-iron production or art museums, you will probably find it after a brief search in the index.

*The Reports of the United States Census* and the *United States Statistical Abstracts* are more specialized, but if you are writing anything about economic conditions, education, or social problems, they are fundamental sources of information.

**Biographical information.** If you are interested in information about important people, there is a whole library of biographical reference books you can use. For American statesmen, writers, and other important people who are no longer living, there is the *Dictionary of American Biography*. For important Englishmen, there is a reference series called the *Dictionary of National Biography*. For living people, such as congressmen, judges, public officials, writers, and so on, there are the various *Who's Who*s. *Who's Who* itself contains information mostly about Englishmen. *Who's Who in America* is the most general biographical reference for living Americans. In addition, there are a lot of specialized books, such as *Who's Who in Education* or *American Men of Science,* which contain information about people in special fields. These books make interesting idle reading. You would be surprised at the number of people you know, in your home town or at your college, who are in these books.

**Encyclopedias.** If you want to work up some specialized topic, like imperialism or Greek mathematics, the place to start is in a good encyclopedia. The best-known American encyclopedia (despite its name) is the *Encyclopaedia Britannica,* but for many purposes other works such as the *Encyclopedia Americana* are equally good or perhaps better. If your library is a large one, you will find an enormous number of encyclopedias from almost every country in every language. An article in an encyclopedia can give you a good general introduction to a topic and sometimes a lot of detail as well. Such articles have well-selected bibliographies, and these make good starters for further reading in the field.

**Books.** If you have to track down some books on a subject, the *United States Catalog* is the place to look. It lists books by author, title, and subject, and it lists all the books published in the United States that are still in print. It is kept up to date with its *Cumulative Book Index* and a regular supplement. If you are looking for an exact citation for a book and know only its author, you will find this source even more convenient than a library catalogue. This is particularly true either if your library is a very small one or if the card catalogue is inconvenient to use.

**Periodicals.** If you're looking for an article in a magazine, journal, or important newspaper, you need the *Reader's Guide to Periodical Literature* and the *International Index of Periodicals*. The *Reader's Guide* covers articles in popular magazines and less technical journals; the *International Index* covers articles in more technical journals in the humanities, arts, and sciences. If articles or editorials in newspapers are what you want, the monthly *New York Times Index* is the source.

**Abstracts.** If you are working in a rather specialized field, you probably should consult its abstracts; these are summaries of articles and books written in the field during any particular year. Such summaries usually go under

**13853.** ROSIN, A., and G. GOLDHABER. The effect of repeated doses of urethane (ethyl carbamate) on the mitotic activity and cellular composition of the bone marrow of normal mice. Blood, Jour. Hematol. 11(11): 1032-1040. Illus. 1956.--A single dose of urethane in normal mice produces a more marked increase in the metaphase index in the bone marrow than does 3 or more daily injections. After 3, 6 and 9 doses an increase in the percentages of ana-and telophases was noted. The percentage of prophases decreased after 6 and 9 doses. Very large promyelocytes, often with prematurely lobated or bizarre shaped nuclei developed and the maturation of segmented leukocytes was augmented. There was damage to the nuclei of erythroid precursors.--R. Isaacs.

**13854.** SCOTHORNE, R. J. (Dept. Anat., U. Glasgow.) The effect of cortisone acetate on the response of the regional lymph node to a skin homograft. Jour. Anat. 90(3): 417-427. 1956.--Cortisone, given systemically in a dosage of 10 mg/day, or applied locally to the surface of the graft in a dosage of 2 mg every 3d day, prolongs the survival of skin homografts and suppresses or reduces the development of the "large lymphoid cell response" in the regional lymph node in rabbits. Cortisone injected subcutaneously between the graft and the regional node in a dosage of 2 mg every 3d day does not prolong homograft survival and does not reduce the "large lymphoid cell response" in the regional node. These findings are consistent with the hypothesis that the large lymphoid cell is actively involved in the production of antibodies against skin homografts. The mechanism of action of cortisone in prolonging survival is discussed, and it is tentatively concluded that cortisone is effective principally by reducing the power of the graft to elicit the immune response.--R. J. Scothorne.

# THE USE OF ABSTRACTS

*Above are sample entries in* Biological Abstracts. *Like the abstracts available in most special fields, they give a brief synopsis of the contents of articles and books. Below is part of a page from the index of* Chemical Abstracts, *illustrating the way you can find abstracts bearing on a particular topic.*

**Mass action,** law of, app. for fitting data to, in enzyme reactions, 779g.
law of, cation-exchange equil. and, 7999e.
law of, condensation and, 7366f.
in metallic-system analysis, 11171h.
**Mass defects.** (See also *Packing.*)
history of, 5568f.
**Masseculites.** (See also *Jaggery.*)
calcn. schemes for, 2398e.
compn. of low-grade, 4237a.
reduction to polyhydric alcs., P 8820a.
viscosity of, detn. of, 4237b.
treatment of—see *Sugar manufacture.*
**Massicot.** See "PbO" under *Lead oxides.*
**Massoia lactone\*,** identity with 5-hydroxy-2-decenoic acid δ-lactone, 14126g.
**Massoy oil.** See *Oils.*
**Mass spectra.** (*For mass spectra of specific elements see the headings for the elements.*)
of alcs. (C₆ and C₇). 3849f.
of benzene monoderivs., 9806b.
of bibenzyl, ethylbenzene and toluene, 4307e
of carbon dioxide isotopic mols., 8025d.
of coal-mine gases, 11757c.
of elementary particles, 8645e.
of ketene and its dimer, 5087g.
of methane mono- and dihalo derivs., 9806d.
of nitrites (aliphatic), 3796h.
of polyat. mols., high-energy ions in, 7425c.
theory of, 11906c.
of s-triazine, 12545f.
**Mass spectrographs.** See *Mass spectrometers.*
**Mass spectrography.** See *Mass spectroscopy.*
**Mass spectrometers, Mass spectrographs.** (See also *Omegatrons.*), P 3148de, 6228i, P 9766e, P 11123i, 13401d.
for analysis of solids, 13463g.
with anastigmatic image, 8644i.

ion abundance ratios by, 6816d.
of ions from field emission microscope, 13405e.
in mineralogy, 3207b.
of nitrogen dioxide in gases, 1890g.
of org. compds. of large mass, 11912f.
of oxidation products of unsatd. hydrocarbons, 12672g.
of pentane pyrolysis, 8003c.
of petroleum fractions, 9660f.
in petroleum industry, 9661d.
of phenol adsorption by catalysts contg. Ni, 13340c.
photographic layer for use in, supported on elec. conductor, P 12562f.
reviews on, 3186d, 9762c, 13401d.
of solids, 9762d.
of solids, with high-frequency spark, 5015f.
of styrene polymer decompn., 5639e.
of sulfur dioxide, neg. ions formed in, 11183d.
trace-element detn. by, 1140e.
**Mass transfer,** in absorption in packed columns, film resistance and, 411a.
in absorption of gases, 5633e.
to air in flow over plate, 12473c.
by air jets in tubes, 9117a.
in ammonia absorption from air by water in rosette-packed column, 4265e.
in ammonia absorption, packing materials and, 6749b.
analogy with heat and momentum transfer, 2424b.
in atomization, 13282d.
book: Chem. Engineering.—Fluid Flow, Heat Transfer and, 12476e.
from bubbles, 1077g.
of carbon dioxide to aq. NaOH or H₂O in wetted-wall columns, 4292c.
in catalytic gaseous reactions, reactor design and, 2424i.
in convection at vertical plates, 1737a.

the title *Biological Abstracts, Chemical Abstracts,* and so on. Each yearly volume has an index, and in it you can look up either a particular subject or the work of an individual author. There you will find, indicated by a series of numbers, all the references published in one year on this topic or by this author. Looking up these numbers in the volume, you will find a complete citation of the article or book and a short summary of what is in it. As you can imagine, these abstracts are indispensable to scholars and research workers. They can be very useful to you too if you learn what they are like and how to use them.

**In general.** You can see by now that it is not too difficult a job to hunt down the most obscure subject in the world if you know how to use a good reference library. The number of books and articles published each year is staggering, but by means of reference books, abstracts, and indexes, you can pinpoint just one particular thing out of this whole mass of material. Learning to use these reference books puts the whole world of printed matter at your disposal and enormously increases your abilities. As a matter of fact, learning to use these special sources is one of the most valuable things you can get from a college education.

## WRITING A PAPER

Now we will say a few words about writing a paper. We'll tell you what a student's paper ought to be like, the steps to be followed in writing the paper, and something about the form it ought to be in.

**Choosing the subject.** Usually you have some freedom in choosing the subject of a paper assigned to you. In the case of themes in English composition, you sometimes have complete freedom to write about anything that interests you. More often, though, you must pick a topic within the limits of the course you are taking.

Selecting a topic is one of the hardest things about writing a paper. If you pick one that is too trivial, too big, too personal, or too con-troversial, you are likely to run into trouble. Most instructors will warn you of the troubles you will have if you choose a topic that is too big or too difficult. You might also be warned about taking a topic that is too limited or one that is too emotionally loaded for you. (The instructor and other people are not likely to share the prejudices you reveal when you write about emotionally loaded or controversial issues.) But better than telling you about the things to avoid would be to tell you about ways to find a good topic.

One of the best ways to find useful and important topics to write about is to thumb through the indexes of textbooks and treatises already written on the subject. Suppose, for example, you are taking a course in human genetics and you want to write a paper about the relationships between race and genetics. Find a book like Boyd's *Genetics and the Races of Man,* and look through the index. The chances are you will find a few entries that will give you some ideas for a paper. Just for practice, why don't you pick up a textbook that is handy and see how many interesting topics for a paper you can find in just a few minutes? Another index you can use to hunt for ideas is one in the abstracts for special fields that we mentioned earlier. The topical indexes in such volumes suggest important and worthwhile topics; by looking up the summaries referred to in the indexes, you can see what articles and books there will be on a particular topic.

For some kinds of papers, of course, this approach won't work, but another one will. One instructor, for example, frequently has his engineering students write articles on the design of common household articles. The student must find something ordinary like a stove, a sink, or a hand tool and describe both what is wrong with it from the engineering point of view and how it might be improved. Here the trick is to find something that really needs improvement. The instructor's purpose is not so much to get the student to redesign something as it is to alert the student to engineering problems in common, everyday things. If you had a topic like this, what would you choose to write about?

The point we are trying to make is that your daily experience is full of things to which you can apply the ideas you have gotten from your academic education. These are frequently excellent topics for term papers.

Another source of ideas for papers is the connection between various subjects you are interested in. Suppose you are a psychology major taking a course in aesthetics. Why not consider a paper on the properties of design and expression in abstract art and the categories psychologists use in projective testing? These kinds of topics are not easy to do, but they nearly always are interesting, both to you and the instructor.

Choosing a topic that probably will be interesting to the instructor is, incidentally, a good ground rule. You can get some hints about his interests from his special area of training and from the things that make him enthusiastic in class. If you aren't too sure about his interests, then at least try to select an important area to write about rather than something so trivial that few people could get interested in it. We make this suggestion not to encourage "apple polishing" but as an instance of the more general principle that you should always consider the interests of your reading audience both in choosing a topic and in working out your approach to it.

**Gathering the material.** After you have chosen a topic, you are ready to gather material. Where you start to do this depends on the subject you are writing about, the length and complexity of the paper, and the type of paper. For some papers, you will need to do very little reading; for others you will have to do a thorough job of library research. The first kind of paper—the kind for which you do little reading—is apt to be a rather individual matter, and we won't say much about that. We can say something, however, about gathering material for a paper with an extensive bibliography.

First of all, you have to get some background for the topic you have chosen. Your instructor probably can help you here, and he can clarify or limit the topic as well as suggest background reading. In many cases, this reading will furnish a bibliography that will lead you to other reading materials. In other cases, you'll have to go to the abstracts or other special bibliographic sources and patiently gather your references. In a few cases, the only thing you can do is to use everything at your command from library card catalogues to periodical indexes.

We have already told you in Chapter Five something about the use of cards for research notes. During the writing of a term paper, using cards is the only way to proceed. You put each reference on one card so that you can arrange and rearrange the cards in any way that you want. From the notes on your cards you can write an outline.

**An outline.** Very few people can write about a complicated topic without an outline. Those who can are able to do so only because they can keep an outline in their heads. In working up an outline, think first of the two, three, or four main divisions, the principal points or topics that you want to cover. The best way to begin is to put these as headings on separate pieces of paper so that you have plenty of space to fill in below. Then under your main headings write the specific points you have in mind. Depending upon how complicated your paper is, you will want to carry the outline out to third- or fourth-order headings. A simple theme will probably be summarized by one or two classes of heading. Under the last order of heading, you can jot down notes and reminders about what to say.

After you begin writing, you will probably find that you want to revise your outline. Do so in such a way that the revised outline can serve as a kind of table of contents for your theme. Indeed, you will want to preserve your outline in the form of headings throughout the paper.

**Writing the paper.** Very few people can get by with just one version of something they write. Usually the first draft is necessary. You will want to write your first draft from your notes on cards arranged in the order of your outline. Try to write it pretty much the way you want the final version to be, but be less concerned about the right way of getting your ideas on paper than about just getting them down. After you have them in front of you, you can work them over more easily.

One important point to remember in writing the first draft is to leave plenty of room for correction. If you type—and you will be much better off if you can type even your first draft— leave at least two spaces between lines and perhaps even three. If you handwrite your first draft, write on only every other line.

After you have written the first draft, go over it once for corrections. Then put it aside for a while. This is an important step. Many students fail to give themselves enough time to write papers so that they must do their drafts and final version all bunched together. Time between the original draft and the final version allows you to get a fresh approach so that a lot of things that were difficult or obscure in the first draft can more easily be corrected.

When you rewrite the paper, be extremely careful. At this stage, be very critical of your spelling, grammar, and punctuation. Ask yourself, "Is what I have written clear, convincing, and interesting?" Here is where a long delay between your original version and your final version is very important. If you allow more than just a few days to go by, you will partly forget what you've written, and you will be better able to read your paper in the way somebody else would read it.

The form of your final version is very important. If at all possible, it should be typed. Also, unless it is a discursive essay on some matter of feeling or opinion, it should be organized into sections. These sections should correspond to the headings in your final outline. All statements should be either carefully documented or clearly indicated as your own. When you cite references (as you must), you should make your citations conform to the usual policy for the subject matter you are writing about. In most subjects, footnotes are used for citation, but in some of the sciences a different system is used. Be very accurate and careful about your citations and especially about quotations. Make sure you clearly set apart all quotations and that the quotations are accurate. Incidentally, in your card-file notes be very careful to indicate where you have quoted. If you don't, you will forget and are likely to take somebody else's words as your own restatement of what that individual said. This can get you into a lot of trouble.

Finally, make a carbon of every important paper you write. Your instructor may want a copy for his files; for this and other reasons two copies will be useful. Sometimes term papers turn out to be of real value. They help people get started on careers. Sometimes they grow into Ph.D. dissertations. And sometimes they are even worth publishing as they stand. Try to make yours be of value to you and other people.

CREUSE
CETTE
CHATTE
FRAÎCHE,

HOMME!

## EIGHT

## STUDYING

## FOREIGN

## LANGUAGES

THE STUDY OF A FOREIGN LANGUAGE presents some rather special problems. Your task isn't just to understand and remember what you read and hear; you must learn the skills of speaking and writing a new language. If you really want to learn a new language, you must work at it until it becomes as familiar to you as the habits of dressing or driving a car. In this chapter, we will suggest some of the ways of working at it that are especially likely to be fruitful. These will be discussed under two general headings: The General Approach and Techniques in Language Study.

### THE GENERAL APPROACH

Different students, of course, will have different problems in studying foreign languages. This is true of all subjects but particularly of languages. Some will find reading the language

relatively easy but understanding the spoken language rather difficult, and vice versa. Some will experience their greatest trouble in composing thoughts in the language, others in translating it. You'll have to find out for yourself just what comes most easily to you and what gives you the greatest difficulty. And in reading the suggestions below, you'll find that some are much more applicable than others to your problems of studying foreign languages.

**Keeping up with the work.** You can fall behind in economics, history, biology, or literature and later catch up on them, though we don't recommend it. You are really in hot water, however, if you fall behind in a foreign language. Consequently, regular, daily preparation of lessons and reading assignments is absolutely necessary, even if you are to do no more than pass in the course.

The reason is that learning a language proceeds in definite steps, just as a baby must stand before it can walk and walk before it can run. You must know the meaning of words before you can use them in simple phrases and sentences. You must know something about word order before you can use words or translate them in more complex sentences. You must know the various forms a word can take before you can get tenses straight and the relationship of words to each other in a clause or sentence. For these reasons, you must keep on schedule, taking the more elementary steps that are prerequisite to the more complicated ones. Otherwise, you'll find you just can't do the next assignment and won't know what is going on in class. Hence, in foreign languages, it is doubly important that you stick to a regular program of study.

**Recitation.** All the steps in the study techniques we have already outlined (Chapter Three) are applicable to the study of language, but one, recitation, is especially important. You can't learn a language without it, and the easiest way to fail a course in foreign language is to neglect it. Indeed, 80 per cent or more of your time, particularly in the early stages of language study, should be spent in recitation.

You know, of course, that you cannot learn a special skill, like tennis, typewriting, or playing the trumpet, without practice. Like playing tennis or typewriting, using a language is a skill, and you can learn to use it only by practice. Therefore, when you tackle a foreign language for the first time, you might as well prepare yourself for some real work. If you approach the language in a half-hearted way, the chances are you're wasting your time. You can never get very far without practice—and practice means recitation.

Actually there are three skills you must master in learning a new language: First of all, you must learn to read it and to translate it into your own language. Secondly, you should learn to understand the language when you hear it. Thirdly, you should learn to speak the language. Most American students are interested in the first skill, but with increased foreign commerce and American personnel in other countries, listening to, and speaking, a language are becoming more and more important. If you emphasize recitation in learning a language, you will be working at all three skills, since all are involved when you recite.

**Learning grammar.** In American colleges, most courses in foreign languages place a lot of stress on grammar. Language teachers try to teach you the structure of a new language so that it becomes second nature to you. If you know the rules of grammar in a language, you can construct sentences of your own in that language as well as understand what other

people say and write in the language.

There are several things that frequently get students into trouble with the grammar of a foreign language. The first is that many students either have forgotten or never knew the rudiments of English grammar. Consequently they are confused when their Spanish or French instructor talks about tenses, moods, possessives, declensions, gerunds, and participles. They find that the grammar of a foreign language is so much nonsense, a complete mystery. The reason is that they do not know the meaning of these grammatical terms in their own language whereas their instructor takes it for granted that they do. If you find yourself in this difficulty in a foreign language, you can make up your deficiencies as you go along with the aid of an ordinary English dictionary and a little work.

Very frequently students encounter grammatical terms for the first time in studying a foreign language. Here is an example: Few students of English grammar are likely to run across an expression like "a noun in the dative case" (or "a pronoun in the accusative case" and so on). This is because meanings in English are customarily given by word positions, English seldom employing special word endings (*case* endings) to show grammatical relations. Yet in many other languages such endings are frequent. Hence it is an advantage to be able to name and talk about the dative case, for instance, which may be indicated by a special ending on nouns and pronouns. There is nothing mysterious about the dative; it is just the indirect object of a verb. In the sentence "He gave me the book," "me" is in the dative case.

Whenever you run across new grammatical terms in a foreign language, make sure that you understand them. You usually can do that best by thinking about what kind of statement in English a particular grammatical term refers to.

Often students diligently memorize the special grammatical categories of a new language without attaching any real meaning to what they memorize. Thus they will learn the declension of a class of German nouns with the example "nominative, *das Haus*; genitive, *des Hauses*; dative, *dem Hause*; and accusative, *das Haus*." Such students can rattle off lists like this for examinations, but when they come to using their understanding of what these different cases mean and how they are used in sentences, they are lost.

One problem with all languages is that they are full of irregularities. Grammarians try to make up rules describing the way all words are used in a language, but there are always exceptions to the rules. Therefore there are irregular nouns and irregular verbs, which do not follow the general rules for either case or conjugation endings. The only thing you can do with these is to memorize them. You must recite them—not only in lists but in phrases and sentences—until they become second nature to you. You'll then be able to employ them in sentences and consistently recognize them when you see them in print.

**Thinking in a language.** Given the right conditions, of course, you don't need to know grammar in order to learn a language. Indeed, everyone learns his native language this way. A baby starts out by learning the meaning of words as they are spoken by others around him and later uses them in sentences, copying from others and being corrected by them. By the time he goes to school and long before he has learned reading or writing, let alone grammar, he has a very good mastery of the language compared with that of the typical student who studies foreign language for a couple of years. All this without grammar and without reading or writing!

The child learns language this way simply because he practices and practices it until he thinks in the language. Unfortunately, it is seldom possible to put college students in the position of the baby, where they are forced to rely exclusively on the language being learned. If language teachers had their way, they would do just this, for they know that living and thinking with a language every hour of the day is the one way to master it quickly and well. In special schools set up for language teachers, military personnel, and others whose chief goal is to master a language, the teaching usually stresses this way of learning.

Although the college student normally can't obtain this kind of training, he can take an important lesson from it. To make the most rapid progress in language study, he can do everything possible to practice it and to use it to think with. He can seek out foreigners who speak the language and converse with them in their tongue. He can secure foreign-language newspapers and read them regularly. He can try to take in foreign movies, which are often running somewhere in the larger cities. At the very least, he can arrange with other students taking his course to set aside periods when they can converse exclusively in the foreign language. In this way, using and understanding the language can gradually become second nature

to him, and he won't have to stumble through it word by word.

To think in a language means not only to be fluent in it and to know it well but something else even more fundamental. It means you don't have to "translate" any more. You come to know the meaning of foreign words and sentences without turning them back into English. After all, you don't read English by translating it; that is to say, you don't turn words into other words to understand them. Rather you have associated these words with objects, events, and qualities so that they have direct meaning for you. This is what you should work toward in studying another language. When you achieve it, you'll understand the foreign words and use them without thinking at all in English. As a consequence, you'll save yourself a lot of work going from the language to English and back again. You'll be master of the language, which is your real goal anyway; and that will give you satisfaction as well as a good grade in the course.

## TECHNIQUES

## IN LANGUAGE STUDY

Because you must walk before you can run, you can't start right off thinking in a language, especially when you must proceed at the relatively slow pace of the typical college course in a foreign language. You must perforce begin thinking in English and translating foreign words into and from English. Only gradually can you abandon translation and come to think in the language. During your progress from one stage to the other, you may find some of the following suggestions helpful.

**Studying by phrases and sentences.**  In the very first few weeks of a course in a foreign language, students nearly always translate word for word. This is all right for the kind of elementary sentences you get at this stage, but it won't do at all when the going gets rougher. Yet many students persist in this word-for-word translation throughout the entire study of a

language. For a language like Spanish this is less likely to get you into trouble (because the grammar and word order are so much like English) than for languages like Latin and German, which have word orders quite different from English ones. A second-year student in German can easily get lost trying to find his way word for word through the seemingly impenetrable thicket of a German sentence, for the German word order is so different that it makes little sense translated literally. The student must learn to think in German word order and get the sense of the sentence as a whole before he looks up the specific words he does not know. And even when he is concentrating on specific words, he must keep in mind the relations between words, the over-all meaning, in order to translate them properly.

You will discover yourself that this is the only way you can translate complicated sentences. If you are doing no better than word-for-word translation, you are in trouble and you need help. We cannot tell you exactly what your difficulties are since they will be different for different people. One frequent difficulty, however, is that the student doesn't have the basic elements of a vocabulary, such as relative pronouns or irregular verbs, so well memorized that they are second nature to him. Other students don't know their syntax or word order well enough to be able to tell where they are in a sentence. This is a particular difficulty for students of German. Thus in a sentence like *Haben Sie den Bauer gesehen, der auf dem Wagen sass?* ("Have you seen the farmer who sat on the wagon?"), a badly confused student may try to translate *der* as a definite article rather than as a relative pronoun. An example of a parallel problem in French is the sentence *Elle a reçu les fleurs que lui ont envoyées des amies* ("She received the flowers that friends sent her"), where the unobservant student may read the objective pronoun *que* as the nominative pronoun *qui,* thus making hash of the sense. By looking over the whole sentence and by relating the words to one another, you would not be able to make a mistake of this kind.

**Dissecting words.** There is, of course, a time and place for paying attention to individual words. One is when you've read a sentence and can't get its meaning because you're not sure of one or more words in it. Another, naturally, is in the process of building your vocabulary. While learning a language, you're always adding to your store of usable words. You'll often find it necessary to look up a word in the dictionary and try to remember it. You'll be saved a lot of work, though, if you try to break words down into their elements and determine the meaning of the elements. We've already suggested that you do this in building an English vocabulary (see page 51), and it is just as appropriate in the study of another language.

Languages are put together in different ways, but most of them, like English, have root words to which other words or parts of words have been attached. If you learn the general meanings of the affixes (prefixes and suffixes), you frequently can figure out a word you've never seen before merely by dissecting it into its root and affixes. Even if you don't get the precise meaning in this way, the process of dissecting the word will help you remember its meaning once you've learned what it is.

**Cognate words.** Remember too that many of the words in European languages are similar to words in English. This is true because English has its historical roots in both the Germanic and Romance (French, Spanish, Italian) languages. Hence many words in these languages have carried over into English. The original forms have often been modified in the process, of course, but they are nevertheless similar in meaning and appearance to their English descendants. If you look for such similar words, called "cognate" words, that have a common heritage, you will find translation much easier.

## THE USE OF COGNATES

*Below are two passages, one in French (from C. T. Morgan,* Psychologie physiologique, *trans. by H. Lesage, Presses Universitaires de France, Paris, 1949, p. 1) and the other in German (from F. G. G. Schmidt,* Berühmte Deutsche neuerer Zeit, *Knopf, New York, 1929, pp. 62, 63). For this exercise, select the passage in a language you have not yet studied. As you read it, have a pencil and paper handy. In one column, write any foreign words that look like English; in a second column, write the English words that are most similar to the foreign words; and in the third column, write your guess about the correct translation of each of the foreign words. When you have finished, turn to page 101 and compare your answers with the lists you find there.*

La physiologie et la psychologie étudient, l'une et l'autre, l'organisme vivant mais chacune de ces deux sciences vise un but différent. La psychologie cherche à comprendre comment les stimuli physiques règlent le comportement de l'organisme. La physiologie, par contre, se propose de comprendre les processus qui se déroulent à l'intérieur de l'organisme.

Paul Ehrlich war geboren am 14 März 1854 in Strehlen (Schlesien). Er besuchte die Elementarschule seiner Vaterstadt, dann das Gymnasium zu Breslau, wo er besonders gut Latein lernte und ausgeprägte mathematische Begabung zeigte. Trotzdem empfand er die Schule stets als Zwang, und für gewisse Fächer besass er nicht das geringste Interesse. Die Prüfungen waren ihm fürchterlich. Wegen der guten Kenntnisse im Lateinischen war ihm schon der Wegfall der mündlichen Prüfung in Aussicht gestellt worden, als ihm „seine einseitige Begabung" einen Streich spielte. In der Schlussprüfung sollte er einen Aufsatz schreiben über das Thema: „Das Leben ein Traum."

To illustrate what we mean, take a pencil and piece of paper and study the sentences given in the accompanying exercise, The Use of Cognates. You'll find you can get pretty close to the meaning of many words in languages you've never studied.

You should be warned, however, that cognates can lead you astray and that you cannot rely blindly on the apparent similarities of foreign and English words. Sometimes a foreign word looks very much like an English word and yet has a rather different meaning. This can happen either by "accident" or because cognate words, words actually having a common beginning, have gradually changed their meaning through centuries of usage. Even when the meanings of cognate words are similar, there may be such fine shades of difference between them that you can't accurately translate them in the most obvious way. It's therefore a good rule to look up all words at least once to check their exact meaning, but only after you've attempted a guess about them based on their apparent similarity to English. In this way, you'll use their cognate relations for recitation and later as a device for remembering more easily their exact meanings.

**Using cards.** As we've pointed out, there is a lot of memorizing in the study of languages, and students have always tried many techniques to make their memorizing easier and more efficient. A common one is to write a foreign word on one side of a card and its translation on the other side. (Indeed, you can buy such cards already printed.) You can test yourself by running through the foreign words while making translations of them. When you're stumped, you remind yourself of the correct translation by flipping the card over on its back. This can be a worthwhile practice if used judiciously.

First of all, you should make up your own cards. You learn by this, and your own cards will be much more useful to you than somebody else's set. Secondly, you should keep your working stack of cards small. Make sure you've thoroughly mastered one set of cards

before you add other ones to the stack. When you're sure of a word, you can throw that card aside. This way you can keep the stack down to manageable size.

When you come to translating more difficult passages, it is a good idea to make up a card every time you must look up a word. If this is all you do, however, you'll soon have a bulging packet of cards. So periodically set aside time to study your cards. Run over them—perhaps once a day. Each time you know the word, put down a tally on the card; each time you don't, put down a zero. When you get up to five tallies in a row without any zeros, the chances are you won't forget the word again. You can then put this card aside.

There is one other way to use cards. As you acquire a reading knowledge of a language and are learning more complicated words and abstract words with many different meanings, it is a good idea to put down whole phrases, not just single words, on your cards. These help you to think in larger units and to use words in their proper context. Context is always the best support for meaning; things you can't remember at all when they are taken by themselves can easily be remembered when you have them associated with other things.

Students sometimes write English words between the lines or on the margins of passages they are translating. This is easier than using cards, but it isn't, as a rule, the best thing to do. It has two disadvantages: (1) It leaves the translation in full view when you are reading the foreign words and thus makes it virtually impossible for you to recite without prompting. It's much better to get the meaning yourself and look at the translation only when you fail— an argument for cards. (2) By focusing your attention on the translation, it tends to keep you thinking in English rather than in the foreign language. Since you eventually want to know the meanings of words without converting them to English, it is better not to refer to English any more than you have to.

**Ponies and trots.** In advanced language classes, where you're reading books or lengthy passages from foreign literature, it is often possible to procure English translations of the material known informally as "ponies" or "trots." In some cases, the trot supplies interlinear translation—English words between the lines of foreign material. In others, the trot consists of the foreign text on one page and the English translation on the facing page. Although in principle such trots should help you learn a language, as they are ordinarily used they are a detriment to progress in language study.

Interlinear translations have the disadvantage we mentioned above for English words written between or near the foreign lines you are reading. They also make life much too easy. The student doesn't have to figure out or look up a translation even once. Hence he deprives himself of the opportunity of recitation and of the precise knowledge of a word he gains by "looking it up." This is also true of trots that give the translation on the facing page, though these permit you to read without looking at the translation if you really want to.

An even more serious objection to the trot is that it handicaps thinking in the language. When you get to the stage where you can use trots, you should be making progress in thinking in the language and you should avoid as much as possible the step of translating the language into English. Trots obviously don't encourage you to think in another language; in fact, they do just the reverse.

A final objection to many trots is that they are such free and easy translations that the student never gets to know the exact meanings of the words and phrases he is reading. Free translation can be very desirable when the translator knows precisely what he is interpreting, but when offered to the person who isn't very skilled in the first place, it is a very poor teacher.

For these reasons, language instructors generally take a rather dim view of trots or similar aids to translation. Some instructors go so far as to fail a student who uses them. On the other hand, there are times when it might be profitable to read an English version of something you are going to translate. The best policy is to follow conscientiously the instructions of your teacher in this matter.

**In general.**    There are a number of special techniques for learning languages as well as different emphases in the teaching of them. Special phonograph records for helping you learn such languages as French, Spanish, and German are generally available in commercial bookstores or can be purchased by mail order. (They're advertised regularly in newspapers and magazines.) If you consider studying with such records and are enrolled in a college language course, you had better ask your instructor about such records and which ones he recommends, if any. His advice in this matter will depend upon the skills he emphasizes in his course and the particular techniques he employs in teaching a foreign language.

Some courses emphasize reading the foreign language; others, speaking it. Some stress grammar while others don't. Some require a very precise understanding of words, and others permit rather free translation. Sometimes special courses are offered in scientific German or scientific French with the purpose of preparing science students only for reading the technical literature in their subject. Your instructor will stress those techniques best suited to the purposes of your particular course.

Some students get very discouraged in studying a foreign language and say they have no aptitude for it. Of course, aptitudes for something like the study of languages differ from individual to individual. Probably, however, a much larger amount of variation among college students, who tend to be rather alike in basic aptitudes, is due to work habits, techniques of study, and background information. Nowhere,

## THE USE OF COGNATES

*The lists below contain most of the cognate words in the passages on page 98. Since similarity of words and their historical origins is to some extent a matter of judgment, your list may be somewhat different and still be a good one. Note how often guesses based on similarities are substantially correct. Also note some instances in which the similarities are misleading.*

| French word | Similar English word | English translation |
|---|---|---|
| *physiologie* | physiology | physiology |
| *psychologie* | psychology | psychology |
| *une* | one | one |
| *autre* | other | other |
| *organisme* | organism | organism |
| *deux* | deuce | two |
| *sciences* | sciences | sciences |
| *différent* | different | different |
| *cherche* | search | aim, search |
| *comprendre* | comprehend | understand, comprehend |
| *comment* | comment | how, in what manner |
| *stimuli* | stimuli | stimuli |
| *physiques* | physics | physical |
| *règlent* | regal | govern |
| *contre* | contrary | on the other hand (with *par*) |
| *propose* | propose | purpose, intend (with *se*) |
| *processus* | processes | processes |
| *déroulement* | roll | unroll, unfold |
| *intérieur* | interior | interior, the inside |

| German word | Similar English word | English translation |
|---|---|---|
| *geboren* | born | born |
| *Elementarschule* | elementary school | primary school |
| *Vaterstadt* | father state | native town |
| *Gymnasium* | gymnasium | high school |
| *gut* | good | good, well |
| *Latein* | Latin | Latin |
| *lernte* | learned | learned |
| *mathematische* | mathematical | mathematical |
| *Schule* | school | school |
| *Interesse* | interest | interest |
| *Prüfung(en)* | proof | examination, test |
| *mündlichen* | monthly | oral |
| *über* | over | concerning (with *schreiben*) |
| *Thema* | theme | subject, theme |
| *Leben* | live | life |
| *Traum* | dream | dream |

except perhaps in mathematics, are things like work habits more important than they are in the study of a foreign language. After all, as Mark Twain remarked, even French babies learn to talk French. Your job is to learn a language, and the only way you can do it is to give yourself a lot of practice. If you think you have a low aptitude for language, you should allow more time for the study of it than almost anything else.

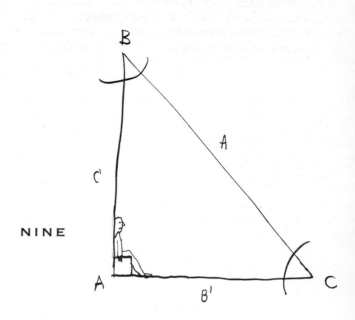

MANY STUDENTS get along all right in their courses as long as the courses do not have anything to do with numbers or mathematics. Many students find chemistry interesting and not too difficult except for the computations they must make; a lot of students get along famously in biology until they come to genetics, which uses mathematical formulas and special computations. And things are getting more and more difficult all the time for such students; nowadays, in courses in psychology, economics, and many other fields in the social sciences, formulas and mathematical reasoning are becoming part of the basic tools for learning. If you have trouble with numbers and formulas, you are doing the wrong thing by trying to avoid contact with them. A little work will help you to deal with these problems much more effectively. You may never become a mathematician, but at least you can learn some of the elementary principles of mathematics and computing.

There is nothing mysteriously difficult about numbers. Many students who do well in mathematics have great difficulty with other things such as languages and literature. Difficulties with one or another tool subject (like mathematics or language) are usually the result of deficiencies in past learning, and you can correct these deficiencies if you try.

**Check your basic skills.** Surveys show that much of the trouble students have with numbers and mathematics arises from deficiencies in elementary skills, the kinds of skill you are supposed to have learned in grammar school

## NINE

# MATHEMATICAL

# PROBLEMS

and high school. Many people never really master these skills, and other people forget them because they don't use them.

On an accompanying page we have listed a few examples of these elementary skills. They are simple problems in basic arithmetic. You will probably wonder what a discussion of addition, subtraction, multiplication, and division is doing in a book written for college students. If so, you might ask yourself whether you can, for example, add and subtract rapidly and without error. Some college students still add by counting to themselves or on their fingers; if you do this, you are in need of some serious drill. If you have a tendency to make mistakes at all, you must be on guard and double-check any simple computations you make.

If you have trouble with long division, addition and subtraction of fractions, multiplication of fractions, and so forth, you might glance at the rules on page 105. Here you will find succinct directions for a lot of these basic skills. If you don't know some of them, practice by working on some examples. If you have trouble with the examples, set up for yourself a program of drill, say, in multiplication and division of fractions. You can find help for such a program in books written specifically for the student who is weak in mathematical skills. You might also ask your science or mathematics teacher for some suggestions.

## ARITHMETIC

In subjects like physics and chemistry, you'll have to do over and over again the kinds of arithmetic we've been talking about. Also in such courses, you'll need other specialized skills; in this section we'll describe some of them.

**Proportions.**   In chemistry, one of the most common computations is in the form of a proportion. A proportion is an equation in which one fraction equals another, but in which you don't know one of the numbers (numerator or denominator) of one of the fractions and must try to find out what it is. In other words, you must find a missing number in one of the fractions. For example, $4/7 = 5/?$. Sometimes the problem is written this way:

$$4 : 7 : : 5 : ?$$

Written in this form, it means "Four is to seven as five is to what?" In general, these names are given to the parts of a proportion:

$$\text{Extreme} : \text{mean} : : \text{mean} : \text{extreme}$$

The rules for solving the proportion and finding the unknown quantity are:

1.  If both extremes and one mean are given, multiply the extremes and divide by the mean.

2.  Or if only one extreme is given and two means are given, multiply the means and divide by the extreme.

If you look at the problem we gave you, rule 2 applies since only one extreme but two means are given. Therefore you would write the problem like this:

$$\frac{7 \times 5}{4} = ?$$

The answer is 8¾.

Try working out some examples of both

## PRACTICE PROBLEMS

*You should be able to perform the following problems rapidly without making any mistakes and without marking the paper except for the answers. If you make mistakes or resort to counting or scratch work, you need drill in the fundamentals of arithmetic (adapted from J. S. Orleans and Julie L. Sperling, "The Arithmetic Knowledge of Graduate Students," Journal of Educational Research, 48:177–186, 1954).*

**Add**

| 3 | 18 | 10 | 18 | 48 | 37 | 11 | 310 |
|---|----|----|----|----|----|----|-----|
| 8 | 6  | 8  | 12 | 5  | 11 | 15 | 22  |
| 6 | 10 | 4  |    | 11 | 11 | 21 | 25  |
|   |    | 4  |    |    |    | 43 |     |

**Subtract**

| 48 | 100 | 54 | 163 | 3.28 | 110.08 | 111.10 |
|----|-----|----|-----|------|--------|--------|
| 15 | 46  | 21 | 93  | 0.05 | 15.71  | 34.21  |

**Multiply**

| | | |
|---|---|---|
| $20 \times 1\frac{1}{4}$ | $15 \times 110$ | $8 \times 33$ |
| $11 \times 0.67$ | $5 \times 1.21$ | $2 \times 216$ |

**Divide**

| | | |
|---|---|---|
| $\dfrac{120}{70}$ | $\dfrac{1.2}{10}$ | $\dfrac{13.6}{50}$ |
| $\dfrac{183}{4}$ | $\dfrac{400}{32}$ | $\dfrac{276}{150}$ |

(**Hint.** $\frac{150}{3} = 50$; $\frac{276}{3} = 92$)

# SOME RULES FOR COMPUTING FRACTIONS

### Definitions

1. A fraction is one or more of the equal parts into which something can be divided. Examples are:

$$\frac{1}{2} \quad \frac{1}{3} \quad \frac{3}{4}$$

2. Fractions are written $\frac{1}{2}$ or $\frac{1}{2}$.

3. The lower number is the *denominator*.

4. The upper number is the *numerator*.

5. *Mixed numbers* are whole numbers and fractions. Examples are:

$$3\frac{1}{2} \quad 2\frac{2}{3}$$

### Adding fractions

1. To add fractions, the denominators must all be the same. Thus $\frac{1}{2}$ and $\frac{1}{3}$ cannot be added until the 2 and 3 are changed.

2. To make the denominators the same, find the *smallest* number (the lowest common denominator) that can be divided evenly by all the denominators. Examples are:

> For 2 and 3, it is 6.
> For 7 and 13, it is 91 ($7 \times 13 = 91$).
> For 2, 8, and 9, it is 72.

*Note.* For many cases, you will have difficulty finding the smallest number by inspection. Find the smallest number into which you can divide as many of the numbers as possible. Then multiply that number by the number you *cannot* divide into it. This will be the lowest common denominator. An example is:

2, 3, 6, 7, 8, 9: All but 7 can be evenly divided into 72. The lowest common denominator is therefore $72 \times 7 = 504$.

3. Multiply the numerator by the number of times the original denominator goes into the lowest common denominator. An example is:

$$\frac{1}{2} + \frac{1}{3} = \frac{1 \times 3}{6} + \frac{1 \times 2}{6} = \frac{3}{6} + \frac{2}{6}$$

4. Add the numerators and place the lowest common denominator as the denominator of the sum. An example is:

$$\frac{3}{7} + \frac{1}{13} = \frac{3 \times 13}{91} + \frac{1 \times 7}{91} = \frac{39}{91} + \frac{7}{91} = \frac{46}{91}$$

5. If the numerator is larger than the denominator, change to a mixed number. An example is:

$$\frac{23}{7} = 3\frac{2}{7}$$

### Subtracting fractions

1. All the rules are the same as for addition except rule 4.

2. For rule 4, subtract instead of add the numerators. An example is:

$$\frac{3}{7} - \frac{1}{13} = \frac{39}{91} - \frac{7}{91} = \frac{32}{91}$$

### Multiplying fractions

1. To multiply fractions, multiply the numerators together and the denominators together. Write the result as a fraction. An example is:

$$\frac{3}{4} \times \frac{5}{7} = \frac{15}{28} \quad \text{or} \quad \frac{5}{6} \times \frac{2}{5} = \frac{10}{30} = \frac{1}{3}$$

2. To multiply a whole number and a fraction, multiply the whole number by the numerator and place the result over the denominator. An example is:

$$5 \times \frac{2}{3} = \frac{10}{3} = 3\frac{1}{3}$$

### Dividing fractions

1. Turn the divisor upside down and multiply. An example is:

$$\frac{4}{9} \div \frac{1}{3} = \frac{4}{9} \times \frac{3}{1} = \frac{12}{9} = 1\frac{3}{9} = 1\frac{1}{3}$$

2. Whole numbers may be written in the form of a fraction with 1 as the denominator. An example is:

$$3 = \frac{3}{1}$$

3. Therefore, to divide a fraction by a whole number, write the whole number as a fraction and invert. An example is:

$$\frac{4}{9} \div 3 = \frac{4}{9} \div \frac{3}{1} = \frac{4}{9} \times \frac{1}{3} = \frac{4}{27}$$

types of problem. If you feel that just a couple of examples let you understand the principles, don't stop there; keep practicing examples until the rules and the procedures become second nature to you.

Another thing you will want to make sure you can do is to translate problems into the correct form. Here is a typical problem in proportions: "A pulley 20 inches in diameter making 300 revolutions per minute is belted to a pulley 15 inches in diameter. What is the speed of the smaller pulley?"

$$15 : 20 : : 300 : ?$$

You set it up this way because the smaller pulley must make *more* revolutions than the larger pulley since it is smaller. Would you have set this problem up the right way?

**Powers and roots.**    A power of a number is gotten by multiplying the number by itself one or more times. Thus 3 squared, or $3^2$, means $3 \times 3$, which is 9. The number of times you multiply gives you the exponent of a number. The exponent in the problem we gave you is 2, and it is written to the right and a little above the number. Exponents can have any value, but the rule is always the same. Thus $3^3$ means $3 \times 3 \times 3$, or 27.

The root of a number is one of the equal numbers that will produce the number you started with when they're multiplied together. Thus the square root of 9 is 3. The sign for a square root is $\sqrt{9}$. (This can also be written $9^{1/2}$.) Just as the power of a number is indicated by an exponent, the number of the root can be shown. For example, the cube (second) root of a number is written $\sqrt[3]{27}$. The answer to this problem is 3.

Squaring numbers is easy, if you know multiplication, but many people have trouble with finding square roots. Fortunately, tables of square roots are readily available; so you usually don't have to do the work of computing (see sample page).

Sometimes you will find powers with negative signs in front of them, like $3^{-2}$. Those of you who remember high-school algebra will rec-

ognize that this is the same thing as $1/3^2$, or $\frac{1}{9}$.

Another difficulty will sometimes face you when you see a problem like this: $3^{1.2}$. How do you multiply a number 1.2 times itself? The way to solve this problem is to resort to logarithms, which are the subject of the next subsection.

**Logarithms.**    Logarithms are a boon to engineers and physicists, for they make it possible to do very involved computations quite easily. If, therefore, you're going to have anything to do with scientific subjects, from physics to statistics, you'd better be acquainted with logs. The logarithm of a given number is the power to which another number (called the "base") must be raised to produce the given number. The base most commonly used is 10. In this case, the logarithm of 100 will be 2 since 10 raised to the second power ($10^2$) is 100. This is generally written

$$\log 100 = 2$$

If you multiply 10 by itself three times you raise it to the third power ($10^3$), and

$$\log 1,000 = 3$$

The logarithms of simple powers of 10 are easy, but what about, say, log 200? Here you have to resort to tables for part of the answer; another part is easy to obtain. The log of 100 is 2, and that of 1,000 is 3; 200 is between 100 and 1,000; so the log of 200 is going to be somewhere between 2 and 3. This is a general principle; the log of 2,000 is somewhere between 3 and 4 (make sure you can tell why).

But what is the exact value of log 200? It is 2.30103. How do you find this? The 2 part, or the easy part, is called the "characteristic," and you can always recognize it as 1 less than the number of places to the left of the decimal in the number you start with. The other part, .30103, is called the "mantissa," and you have to look it up in tables. We won't give you a complete log table; but you can find one very easily, and you will need one if you are going to do any complicated computing. A part of a log table is on page 108. What you do is look

# FINDING SQUARES AND SQUARE ROOTS

*Here is a sample page from a table of squares and square roots. Note how easy it is to find the appropriate answer. For very large numbers whose roots are to be extracted, you work backward from the column of squares and, if necessary, interpolate between the numbers in the table (from Herbert Sorensen, Statistics for Students of Psychology and Education, McGraw-Hill, New York, 1936, p. 348).*

| Number | Square | Square root | Number | Square | Square root |
|--------|--------|-------------|--------|--------|-------------|
| 721 | 51 98 41 | 26.8514 | 761 | 57 91 21 | 27.5862 |
| 722 | 52 12 84 | 26.8701 | 762 | 58 06 44 | 27.6043 |
| 723 | 52 27 29 | 26.8887 | 763 | 58 21 69 | 27.6225 |
| 724 | 52 41 76 | 26.9072 | 764 | 58 36 96 | 27.6405 |
| 725 | 52 56 25 | 26.9258 | 765 | 58 52 25 | 27.6586 |
| 726 | 52 70 76 | 26.9444 | 766 | 58 67 56 | 27.6767 |
| 727 | 52 85 29 | 26.9629 | 767 | 58 82 89 | 27.6948 |
| 728 | 52 99 84 | 26.9815 | 768 | 58 98 24 | 27.7128 |
| 729 | 53 14 41 | 27.0000 | 769 | 59 13 61 | 27.7308 |
| 730 | 53 29 00 | 27.0185 | 770 | 59 29 00 | 27.7489 |
| 731 | 53 43 61 | 27.0370 | 771 | 59 44 41 | 27.7669 |
| 732 | 53 58 24 | 27.0555 | 772 | 59 59 84 | 27.7849 |
| 733 | 53 72 89 | 27.0740 | 773 | 59 75 29 | 27.8029 |
| 734 | 53 87 56 | 27.0924 | 774 | 59 90 76 | 27.8209 |
| 735 | 54 02 25 | 27.1109 | 775 | 60 06 25 | 27.8388 |
| 736 | 54 16 96 | 27.1293 | 776 | 60 21 76 | 27.8568 |
| 737 | 54 31 69 | 27.1477 | 777 | 60 37 29 | 27.8747 |
| 738 | 54 46 44 | 27.1662 | 778 | 60 52 84 | 27.8927 |
| 739 | 54 61 27 | 27.1846 | 779 | 60 68 41 | 27.9106 |
| 740 | 54 76 00 | 27.2029 | 780 | 60 84 00 | 27.9285 |
| 741 | 54 90 81 | 27.2213 | 781 | 60 99 61 | 27.9464 |
| 742 | 55 05 64 | 27.2397 | 782 | 61 15 24 | 27.9643 |
| 743 | 55 20 49 | 27.2580 | 783 | 61 30 89 | 27.9821 |
| 744 | 55 35 36 | 27.2764 | 784 | 61 46 56 | 28.0000 |
| 745 | 55 50 25 | 27.2947 | 785 | 61 62 25 | 28.0179 |
| 746 | 55 65 16 | 27.3130 | 786 | 61 77 96 | 28.0357 |
| 747 | 55 80 09 | 27.3313 | 787 | 61 93 69 | 28.0535 |
| 748 | 55 95 04 | 27.3496 | 788 | 62 09 44 | 28.0713 |
| 749 | 56 10 01 | 27.3679 | 789 | 62 25 21 | 28.0891 |
| 750 | 56 25 00 | 27.3861 | 790 | 62 41 00 | 28.1069 |
| 751 | 56 40 01 | 27.4044 | 791 | 62 56 81 | 28.1247 |
| 752 | 56 55 04 | 27.4226 | 792 | 62 72 64 | 28.1425 |
| 753 | 56 70 09 | 27.4408 | 793 | 62 88 49 | 28.1603 |
| 754 | 56 85 16 | 27.4591 | 794 | 63 04 36 | 28.1780 |
| 755 | 57 00 25 | 27.4773 | 795 | 63 20 25 | 28.1957 |
| 756 | 57 15 36 | 27.4955 | 796 | 63 36 16 | 28.2135 |
| 757 | 57 30 49 | 27.5136 | 797 | 63 52 09 | 28.2312 |
| 758 | 57 45 64 | 27.5318 | 798 | 63 68 04 | 28.2489 |
| 759 | 57 60 81 | 27.5500 | 799 | 63 84 01 | 28.2666 |
| 760 | 57 76 00 | 27.5681 | 800 | 64 00 00 | 28.2843 |

## USING A TABLE OF LOGARITHMS

*Find the first three digits of your number in the left-hand column, then move across the row to the column headed by the fourth digit of your number. The entry is your mantissa. You supply the characteristic by counting one less than the number of digits to the left of the decimal point. If your number has less than three digits, add zeros to bring it up to three and look up the mantissa in the zero column. Below is a sample section of a table of logarithms (from Myron F. Rosskopf, Harold D. Aten, and William D. Reeve,* Mathematics: . . . , *McGraw-Hill, New York, 1955, p. 411).*

### Table of Five-Place Mantissas

| No. | 0 | 1 | 2 | 3 | 4 | 5 | 6 | 7 | 8 | 9 | Proportional parts | |
|---|---|---|---|---|---|---|---|---|---|---|---|---|
| **250** | 39 794 | 811 | 829 | 846 | 863 | 881 | 898 | 915 | 933 | 950 | | **18** |
| 251 | 967 | 985 | *002 | *019 | *037 | *054 | *071 | *088 | *106 | *123 | 1 | 1.8 |
| 252 | 40 140 | 157 | 175 | 192 | 209 | 226 | 243 | 261 | 278 | 295 | 2 | 3.6 |
| 253 | 312 | 329 | 346 | 364 | 381 | 398 | 415 | 432 | 449 | 466 | 3 | 5.4 |
| 254 | 483 | 500 | 518 | 535 | 552 | 569 | 586 | 603 | 620 | 637 | 4 | 7.2 |
| 255 | 654 | 671 | 688 | 705 | 722 | 739 | 756 | 773 | 790 | 807 | 5 | 9.0 |
| 256 | 824 | 841 | 858 | 875 | 892 | 909 | 926 | 943 | 960 | 976 | 6 | 10.8 |
| 257 | 993 | *010 | *027 | *044 | *061 | *078 | *095 | *111 | *128 | *145 | 7 | 12.6 |
| 258 | 41 162 | 179 | 196 | 212 | 229 | 246 | 263 | 280 | 296 | 313 | 8 | 14.4 |
| 259 | 330 | 347 | 363 | 380 | 397 | 414 | 430 | 447 | 464 | 481 | 9 | 16.2 |
| **260** | 497 | 514 | 531 | 547 | 564 | 581 | 597 | 614 | 631 | 647 | | **17** |
| 261 | 664 | 681 | 697 | 714 | 731 | 747 | 764 | 780 | 797 | 814 | 1 | 1.7 |
| 262 | 830 | 847 | 863 | 880 | 896 | 913 | 929 | 946 | 963 | 979 | 2 | 3.4 |
| 263 | 996 | *012 | *029 | *045 | *062 | *078 | *095 | *111 | *127 | *144 | 3 | 5.1 |
| 264 | 42 160 | 177 | 193 | 210 | 226 | 243 | 259 | 275 | 292 | 308 | 4 | 6.8 |
| 265 | 325 | 341 | 357 | 374 | 390 | 406 | 423 | 439 | 455 | 472 | 5 | 8.5 |
| 266 | 488 | 504 | 521 | 537 | 553 | 570 | 586 | 602 | 619 | 635 | 6 | 10.2 |
| 267 | 651 | 667 | 684 | 700 | 716 | 732 | 749 | 765 | 781 | 797 | 7 | 11.9 |
| 268 | 813 | 830 | 846 | 862 | 878 | 894 | 911 | 927 | 943 | 959 | 8 | 13.6 |
| 269 | 975 | 991 | *008 | *024 | *040 | *056 | *072 | *088 | *104 | *120 | 9 | 15.3 |
| **270** | 43 136 | 152 | 169 | 185 | 201 | 217 | 233 | 249 | 265 | 281 | | **16** |
| 271 | 297 | 313 | 329 | 345 | 361 | 377 | 393 | 409 | 425 | 441 | 1 | 1.6 |
| 272 | 457 | 473 | 489 | 505 | 521 | 537 | 553 | 569 | 584 | 600 | 2 | 3.2 |
| 273 | 616 | 632 | 648 | 664 | 680 | 696 | 712 | 727 | 743 | 759 | 3 | 4.8 |
| 274 | 775 | 791 | 807 | 823 | 838 | 854 | 870 | 886 | 902 | 917 | 4 | 6.4 |
| 275 | 933 | 949 | 965 | 981 | 996 | *012 | *028 | *044 | *059 | *075 | 5 | 8.0 |
| 276 | 44 091 | 107 | 122 | 138 | 154 | 170 | 185 | 201 | 217 | 232 | 6 | 9.6 |
| 277 | 248 | 264 | 279 | 295 | 311 | 326 | 342 | 358 | 373 | 389 | 7 | 11.2 |
| 278 | 404 | 420 | 436 | 451 | 467 | 483 | 498 | 514 | 529 | 545 | 8 | 12.8 |
| 279 | 560 | 576 | 592 | 607 | 623 | 638 | 654 | 669 | 685 | 700 | 9 | 14.4 |
| **280** | 716 | 731 | 747 | 762 | 778 | 793 | 809 | 824 | 840 | 855 | | **15** |
| 281 | 871 | 886 | 902 | 917 | 932 | 948 | 963 | 979 | 994 | *010 | 1 | 1.5 |
| 282 | 45 025 | 040 | 056 | 071 | 086 | 102 | 117 | 133 | 148 | 163 | 2 | 3.0 |
| 283 | 179 | 194 | 209 | 225 | 240 | 255 | 271 | 286 | 301 | 317 | 3 | 4.5 |
| 284 | 332 | 347 | 362 | 378 | 393 | 408 | 423 | 439 | 454 | 469 | 4 | 6.0 |
| 285 | 484 | 500 | 515 | 530 | 545 | 561 | 576 | 591 | 606 | 621 | 5 | 7.5 |
| 286 | 637 | 652 | 667 | 682 | 697 | 712 | 728 | 743 | 758 | 773 | 6 | 9.0 |
| 287 | 788 | 802 | 818 | 834 | 849 | 864 | 879 | 894 | 909 | 924 | 7 | 10.5 |
| 288 | 939 | 954 | 969 | 984 | *000 | *015 | *030 | *045 | *060 | *075 | 8 | 12.0 |
| 289 | 46 090 | 105 | 120 | 135 | 150 | 165 | 180 | 195 | 210 | 225 | 9 | 13.5 |
| **290** | 240 | 255 | 270 | 285 | 300 | 315 | 330 | 345 | 359 | 374 | | **14** |
| 291 | 389 | 404 | 419 | 434 | 449 | 464 | 479 | 494 | 509 | 523 | 1 | 1.4 |
| 292 | 538 | 553 | 568 | 583 | 598 | 613 | 627 | 642 | 657 | 672 | 2 | 2.8 |
| 293 | 687 | 702 | 716 | 731 | 746 | 761 | 776 | 790 | 805 | 820 | 3 | 4.2 |
| 294 | 835 | 850 | 864 | 879 | 894 | 909 | 923 | 938 | 953 | 967 | 4 | 5.6 |
| 295 | 982 | 997 | *012 | *026 | *041 | *056 | *070 | *085 | *100 | *114 | 5 | 7.0 |
| 296 | 47 129 | 144 | 159 | 173 | 188 | 202 | 217 | 232 | 246 | 261 | 6 | 8.4 |
| 297 | 276 | 290 | 305 | 319 | 334 | 349 | 363 | 378 | 392 | 407 | 7 | 9.8 |
| 298 | 422 | 436 | 451 | 465 | 480 | 494 | 509 | 524 | 538 | 553 | 8 | 11.2 |
| 299 | 567 | 582 | 596 | 611 | 625 | 640 | 654 | 669 | 683 | 698 | 9 | 12.6 |
| **300** | 712 | 727 | 741 | 756 | 770 | 784 | 799 | 813 | 828 | 842 | | |
| No. | 0 | 1 | 2 | 3 | 4 | 5 | 6 | 7 | 8 | 9 | Proportional parts | |

up the number given (200) and find the mantissa in the table. For other numbers in the 200s, say, 263, there will be a different mantissa, but the characteristic is the same. The log of 263 is 2.41996. Written in exponents, 263 would be $10^{2.41996}$

Suppose you want to find log 2.63. You know that the log of 10 is 1; so the characteristic of log 2.63 is going to be 0 (1 less than the number of digits to the left of the decimal in 2.63). The mantissa is exactly the same as in 263. This makes an important point about reading log tables: The mantissa is always the same if the specific digits are the same. Thus the mantissas of 2,630, 263, or 2.63 are all the same. The complete log for 2.63 is 0.41996.

What about log 0.263? The principle, of course, is exactly the same. But the log will be less than zero, and it makes some special problems because of negative numbers. The log of 0.263 is usually written $9.41996 - 10$. If you are going to deal with problems involving logarithms of numbers less than 1, you should get a copy of a textbook in algebra and study the section on logarithms. If you have been able to understand this brief discussion of logarithms, you should have no trouble with a complete textbook account of logarithms.

You can do lots of computing with logs, and that is one of their values. For example, if you want to multiply two long numbers together, you can find it by adding their logs (this is what a slide rule does for you). Thus $200 \times 263$ can be given by finding the sum of the logs, which is 4.72099. By looking up (backward) in a log table the antilogarithm of 4.72099, you find the product of 200 and 263, or 52,600. The antilog is the number corresponding to a logarithm.

Now we are ready to show you how to find $3^{1.2}$. The rule is as follows: To find the power of any number, multiply the log of that number by the power and find the antilog of the result. Thus $3^{1.2}$ can be found by writing $1.2 \times \log 3$. This gives $1.2 \times 0.47712$, or 0.572544. Since some log tables go to five places only, you might have to round off the last number and look up the antilog of 0.57254. The answer

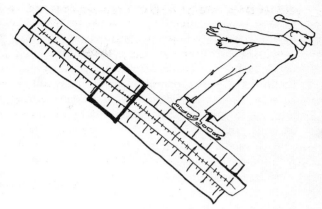

will be 3.74 (rounding off). Thus $3^{1.2} = 3.74$ (approximately).

The purpose of this section has not been merely to show you how to use logs but to show you that their principle is not hard to understand. If you have been avoiding logarithms all your life, you might get hold of a mathematics text and try learning about them.

**The slide rule.** Logarithms are employed in a useful device known as the slide rule, or "slip stick." This, in its simplest form, consists of two "rulers" marked off on logarithmic scales so that the distances between each mark on the scale are relatively the same as the logarithms of the numbers on the scale. Because you add logarithms when you wish to multiply their antilogs and subtract them when you wish to divide, the slide rule enables you to multiply and divide simply by adding and subtracting the numbers on the two scales. This you do by sliding one scale along next to the other.

Because you can do multiplication and division so easily and accurately on a slide rule and because every college student must sometimes carry out such computations, we believe no student should be without a slide rule. There are all kinds of slide rule for different purposes. The simpler ones are relatively inexpensive; the more complicated ones can run up to $10 or $20. If you're not a science student and not likely to do a great many computations other than simple multiplication and division, one of the simpler ones will do. The more elaborate slide rules let you compute answers involving special functions, like the sines and tangents of angles. If you are a science or engineering student, you should get one of the special models designed for your particular field. The instructor in the course concerned can probably suggest the proper model to buy. You can learn how to use your particular slide rule by reading carefully the instructions that come with the rule. In some mathematics books, you'll find instructions for the many "tricks" you can do with the more complicated rules.

**Significant figures.** Whenever you carry out any computations with numbers, you always have to decide how many numbers to use, both when you start solving your problem and as you proceed through its various steps. Where decimals are concerned, this is the question of whether you carry figures to the second, third, or $n$th decimal place. Also, in dealing with large quantities, like the distance of the sun from the earth or the speed of electricity, how many digits should you use and how should you round off your answer? To decide such a question you need to know how many digits in your number are significant, which is to say, how many are reasonably trustworthy and which ones are rather doubtful.

If you're making a measurement in an experiment or exercise, the rule is to record no more than one doubtful figure. If, for example, you're making a measurement with such a crude instrument as an ordinary meter stick, you would probably record your result to two places, for example, 4.2 meters, for you'd be quite sure it was nearer to 4 than to 3 or 5, but you wouldn't be so sure that it was nearer to 4.2 than to 4.1 or 4.3. By writing 4.2, you indicate that you are sure of 4 but somewhat doubtful about the .2 and consider any digits beyond .2 as meaningless. If you had a more accurate metric measure, graduated in centimeters as well as decimeters, you might express the same measure as 4.22 meters since you are now sure of 4.2 but doubtful about the digit representing centimeters.

There is a rule too for the addition, subtraction, multiplication, and division of significant numbers. You shouldn't write digits beyond the first column that contains a doubtful figure. Thus if you add 4.0 pounds of dirt to 3.4365 pounds of gold, the result would be 7.4 pounds of mixture. When your certainty about the weight of dirt doesn't go beyond 4 pounds, the accuracy of the weight of gold is of no use to you, for you can be no more certain about the total than you are about the component with the least certainty. (Remember "A chain is no stronger than its weakest link"?)

When you are multiplying or dividing numbers, you follow the same principle. In this case, it dictates that you carry out the operation to no more figures than are in the one that has the fewer significant figures. If, for example, you multiply 4.0 feet by 6.273 feet (assuming that 4.0 represents all the significant figures), your answer is 25, not 25.0920, for you had only two significant digits in 4.0 and you should have no more than this in your answer.

When you drop figures or round them off to the proper number of significant figures, you follow the rule of raising any digit by 1 when it is followed by more than 5, otherwise leaving it unchanged. For example, to round off 7.46639 to two significant figures, you end up with 7.5; if the number were 7.4499, you would have 7.4. (There's a special rule for rounding a digit followed by 5: If the digit is odd, raise it by 1; if it is even, drop the 5 without changing the digit.)

These rules have two important consequences: First, they keep you from fooling yourself about the precision of your measurements and calculations; dropping figures that aren't significant is merely a matter of getting rid of numbers you can't trust anyway. Secondly, they save you needless work and reduce the possibility of error involved in handling unnecessarily long strings of numbers.

## ALGEBRA

Most students are familiar with the elementary operations of algebra, but it would be well to refresh your memory so that you will recognize them not just in a course in mathematics but any place you may need to use them.

**Negative numbers.** In arithmetic, we use a minus sign to mean subtraction. Thus when you see

$$\begin{array}{r} 100 \\ -\ 25 \\ \hline \end{array}$$

you know that you are to subtract the 25 from the 100. In algebra, however, the minus sign is used to indicate numbers whose values are less than zero. These are negative numbers. Everyone is acquainted with negative numbers because they turn up in weather reports. When we read that the temperature was $-8$ in Chicago yesterday, this means that it was 8° below zero. The negative numbers increase in the opposite direction from positive numbers:

$$-5 \quad -4 \quad -3 \quad -2 \quad -1 \quad 0 \quad 1 \quad 2 \quad 3 \quad 4 \quad 5$$

There are lots of ways in which negative numbers can be used. For example, if I owe $15 more than I have, I might say that my assets are $-$15.

Be careful when you add and subtract negative numbers, for it is very easy to add them when you're supposed to be subtracting them and vice versa. If you look at the series of numbers above, you'll see that the difference between $-3$ and 2 is 5, not 1. Not so obvious perhaps is the fact that $-3$ subtracted from 2 is 5, not $-5$, and 2 subtracted from $-3$ is $-5$, not $(+)5$.

**Addition and subtraction.** The rules for the algebraic addition and subtraction of numbers, or the addition and subtraction of negative *and* positive numbers, are very simple, and they should cause you no trouble if you are careful. Here they are:

1. If all the numbers in a problem are entirely negative or entirely positive, the ordinary rules of arithmetic will do. You add their values for addition and find the difference for subtraction.
2. To add two numbers opposite in sign (one

positive and the other negative), you find the difference between them and give the answer the sign of the larger number. Thus if you want to add 3 and $-7$, the answer is $-4$. Suppose you won $3 at the race track, but you had to pay $7 to get there and get in. You're out $4. Or to put it another way, the algebraic sum of your winnings and expenses at the race track is $-$4.

3. To subtract numbers opposite in sign, change the sign of the number to be subtracted and then add. Thus the difference between 8 and $-3$ is 11. For example, if the temperature is 8° this morning in Chicago and $-3$° in Minneapolis, it is 11° colder in Minneapolis than in Chicago. This is algebraic subtraction. *Note.* If you want to find the difference between two positive numbers, the rule is the same: The difference between 13 and 8 is 5; you have changed the sign of 8 and added algebraically. Likewise, the difference between 12 and 16 is 4 ($-12$ and 16).

4. If you must add a series of numbers which have different signs, you separately find the simple sums of the positive numbers and the negative numbers and then find the *algebraic* sum of these two. Thus if you wish to add $-5$, 3, $-1$, 6, $-2$, $-7$, and 8, you would find the sum of $-5$, $-1$, $-2$, and $-7$, which is $-15$, and the sum of 3, 6, and 8, which is 17. The sum of $-15$ and 17 is 2.

The operations of algebraic addition and subtraction are very easy but students sometimes have difficulty realizing when these operations should be applied. Watch out for problems in which numbers can be both positive and negative; then make sure you are solving these problems the right way.

**Multiplication and division.** If you are going to take elementary physics or statistics, you had better brush up on a few other fundamental operations in algebra. You should get a high-school textbook in algebra and assure yourself that you can add and subtract polynomials (expressions like $2x - y$, which have two or more terms), that you can do algebraic multiplication and division, and that you can solve equations for numerical values.

This last point is especially important, and most simple problems involve only two elementary rules: (1) You can move any term preceded by a plus or minus sign to the opposite side of an equation by changing its sign; and (2) when a term is to be divided into one side of an equation, it can be moved to the other side and used to multiply. Thus for rule 1,

$$30 - x = 5$$
$$- x = 5 - 30$$
$$- x = - 25$$
$$x = 25$$

For rule 2,

$$\frac{x}{10} = 5$$
$$x = 5 \times 10$$
$$x = 50$$

You will have occasion in courses like elementary physics to solve simple simultaneous equations. You use such equations when you must solve for two unknowns. By reading over the section on simultaneous equations in a high-school algebra book, you can brush up on the rules for handling them.

Elementary trigonometry is something else that you will find useful for introductory physics and similar subjects. At the very least, you should make certain that you know and can use properly the ratios that exist among the sides of a right triangle, that is, the trigonometric functions. These ratios are quantities such as the sine and cosine.

None of these things are really difficult. If you have been able to understand the last few pages of this book, you will have no real problems with any kind of elementary mathematics, such as trigonometry or college algebra. Many students are so fearful of mathematics and numbers that they never give themselves a fair chance to find out how well they can do at them.

## DOING PROBLEMS

If you know a little bit about mathematics, you were probably impatient as you read through the preceding section. Now, however, we are coming to some points on the solution of problems that should be useful to everyone. In this section, we will make some suggestions for your mode of attack on problems you'll encounter in your study routine.

**"Homework" problems.**   First and most important: *Do* all assigned problems. Some students don't because, they say, their instructors don't grade them on their daily problems. Even if no one checks you on your daily work, you will be graded on your examination problems, and the only way to prepare for these so that you solve them accurately in the time you are allowed is to do your daily assignments religiously. If you keep working problems as part of your daily routine, you will have no difficulty at examination time. Nor will you have to resort to the excuse that the instructor sprung some "trick questions" on you.

A problem is really a question. We've already seen how valuable questions are in learning. Problems are therefore important to learning too—not just hurdles to overcome. Problems are your opportunities to apply what you have learned and to test yourself about how much you know about what you have been studying. If you have problems assigned in a textbook or a laboratory manual, you should welcome the opportunity to use them in effective study.

When you have studied a particular assignment and are ready to tackle the problems in it, your first task is to make sure you understand the problem. For any particular problem, you must understand what information you are already supposed to know or be able to find quickly and what it is you are trying to find out. To do this, always keep in mind that there is a model for every problem. A model is like a mold; if you can fit your problem into the proper mold, you can easily solve it. To illustrate this, we will take a simple problem in elementary chemistry.

The problem is the following: If you are making carbon dioxide and start with 24 grams of carbon, how many grams of carbon dioxide can you make? If you know a little chemistry, the correct model, or mold, for this problem will immediately occur to you. The model is $C + O_2 = CO_2$. The next step is to put the correct numbers into the model to solve the problem. The person who would give you such a problem would assume you have learned what you need to solve it or at least that you know where to go to find this information. For this problem the information is the atomic weights of carbon and oxygen. These happen to be 12 and 16. You can now set up a proportion: $24/12 = ?/44$. The problem gives you 24 grams of carbon, and you supply the 12 and the 44 for the relative weights of carbon and carbon dioxide (the 44 comes from the combination of 12 for carbon and two times 16 for the oxygen). By solving the proportion, you get the answer, 88.

The problem illustrates the three steps essential in solving problems: First you must have the correct model, or mold, for solving the problem. This you should know from having mastered the relevant material. Then you put into the model the information given in the problem and the other information you may obtain from studying the book or your lecture notes. Finally you solve for some unknown.

To find the proper model for a problem and to check yourself when you think you have chosen the proper model, take advantage of the examples usually supplied in books. Some problems already worked out for you appear in practically all science and engineering books. These can provide models for first working assigned problems and later for solving problems on examinations.

When we say, however, that there is a model for every problem, we don't mean that you can or should always take one that is already made for you. Models are derived from laws and principles; you should always understand the principles underlying any model you use. Some-

times you'll have to make your own model by formulating the problem in terms of principles you've learned and by setting up your own formula or diagram for solving the problem. In elementary courses you'll usually be given examples or specific formulas that will serve as models for solving your problems, but in more advanced courses you may be asked to develop the proper model or formula for solving them. This you will be able to do if you understand the underlying principles. In any case, you are better off and can remember the model better if you make sure you understand the rationale of any model you use.

**Examination problems.** If you work all the problems in daily assignments but still complain that those on examinations are "different" or trick problems, it means that you just aren't prepared for all the changes that can be made in a problem to make it look different.

For example, in the illustration we took from elementary chemistry, there are several ways of putting this same problem: Instead of asking how much carbon dioxide can be made from so much carbon, you can ask how much carbon dioxide can be made with so much oxygen or how much carbon or oxygen it would take to produce a given amount of carbon dioxide. These are all different ways of putting the same problem. You use the same model and the same information. The only difference is in where the unknown appears in the proportion.

To prepare yourself for problems that are different (to learn how to get around trick questions!), practice turning problems around. Take some sample problems and ask yourself how many different ways the same problem can be put. Write out the possible alternatives. If you do this frequently, you will find that you will not be surprised so often on examinations.

Of course, another way to pose similar problems is to switch the elements referred to. You might, for example, get an examination problem about sulfuric acid rather than carbon dioxide. If you are prepared for such possible switches, you will not be in difficulty. You can do that by making lists of the specific things that can be changed in any problem without changing the model.

By the time, for example, that you've encountered the carbon dioxide problem, you probably have already covered a series of reactions such as the making of sulfuric acid, sodium hydroxide, water, and so on. Jot down a list of these and then make sure that you know the models (in this case, reaction equations) and the numbers (atomic weights). If you do this, you should be prepared for all the instructor can fairly ask you.

One of the hazards of examinations consisting of problems is that they require you to work fast. Students taking such examinations are forever finding that they manage to complete only a third or half of the problems they are supposed to do. Or if they do manage to finish the whole examination, they make trivial mistakes in arithmetic. The consequences are often disastrous, for the instructor generally gives credit only for the problems completed correctly; and the difference between the slow student and the fast one or between the inaccurate and the accurate one may be a difference between a failure and an A. Speed and speed with accuracy are more important in problem-type examinations than in any other.

Time can be lost because the student doesn't have the basic skills to do his work correctly and quickly. It can be lost because *he* is lost trying to understand what the problem is about. If the student improves in these respects, he can manage to do more problems accurately in an examination. In addition, however, students are often too slow because they haven't practiced working fast.

The best way to meet this difficulty is to do homework assignments as if they were examinations. When you get ready to do a problem, time yourself as you work fast. Later, you can check yourself at a more leisurely pace. The important point, as in the case of reading faster, is to practice working faster. If you do, you'll find you don't lumber along so slowly and you will feel at home taking an examination.

This brings us to the matter of planning the time allotted to you for taking an examination. Always survey an examination before you start. If you have any choices, decide in advance which problems you will work. Estimate how much time you should spend on each, and keep track of the time to guard against spending too much time on any one problem. Work the easy problems first, leaving the hard ones for last.

In problem-type examinations it is especially important that you leave a little time to check your answers. If a lot of computation is involved, leave enough time to check it thoroughly. This can turn up trivial mistakes that could prevent you from making a good showing on the examination.

## USING GRAPHS AND TABLES

To solve many problems you encounter, you'll need to use a graph or a table. In fact, you need to do this merely to read and understand many of your assignments in the natural and social sciences. Hence it is essential that you know how to use graphs and tables.

**Graphs.** The very simplest graphs are bar graphs that show, by the height of their columns, the number or amount of some particular quantity. One bar might give the government budget for 1950, another for 1951, and so on up to the present. Graphs of this kind convey information quickly and give you a more vivid impression of something than you can get by reading numbers. For that reason, they are used widely in nontechnical magazines and newspapers. They are usually not much use, though, in the solution of problems.

For this purpose, the graph you use is more likely to be a line representing a functional relationship between two variables. The graph, in other words, will say the same thing as an equation and will give the results of working out the equation for a number of different values of each variable. In the accompanying graph, for example, the straight line represents the equation $y = a + bx$, where $a = 2$ and $b = \frac{1}{2}$. If you have any calculations to do with such an equation, you can read the answers off

# READING A GRAPH

*Each line represents an equation. For any given equation, you can find the value of y that corresponds to any value of x. Note that the constant a determines where the line will intercept y when x = 0 and that b determines the slope of the line.*

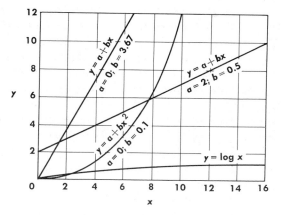

merely by consulting the graph. If you want to know what $y$ equals when $x = 2$, look on the graph and you'll see quickly that the answer is 3. You can do the same thing with any other value of $x$.

Notice how the graph is set up. The value of $x$ is found along the horizontal axis, called the "abscissa," and the value of $y$ is found along the vertical axis, called the "ordinate." To find an answer, you locate the value of $x$ on the abscissa, then erect an imaginary line from that point upward until it intersects the line, which in this case is a straight line, and then finally run an imaginary line horizontally across to the ordinate. The corresponding value of $y$ is your answer. Although the line in the graph may be any shape from straight to complexly curved, this simple operation is the same in reading all rectangular graphs.

Note that $x$ is laid out on the abscissa and $y$ on the ordinate. This is a custom among scientists, but it is an important one because there is usually a reason for it. Most of the time, when you wish to represent the relation between two variables, one of the variables is an *independent variable,* the other a *dependent variable.* The independent variable in an experiment or series of measurements is the one the experi-

menter varies or has control of—the variable whose value he can set—and the dependent variable is the one he measures or lets "depend" on the independent variable.

In the carbon dioxide problem above, the independent variable is the amount of carbon you start with—the amount you use—and the dependent variable is the amount of carbon dioxide you get out of the process. If you wanted to, you could set up a graph for this problem that would let you read off the amount of carbon dioxide you'd get by starting with any amount of carbon. The formula would be $y = a + bx$, where $a = 0$, $b = \frac{44}{12} = 3.67$, $x$ = amount of carbon, and $y$ = amount of carbon dioxide (see graph). You could work out the equation twice, once for 12 grams of carbon dioxide and again for some other amount like 36 grams, plot these two points on your graph, and then draw a line passing through the two points. Thereafter, by using the graph, you could solve the problem for any amount of carbon.

The important point is that we have a convention for plotting the independent variable on the $x$ axis (abscissa) and the dependent variable on the $y$ axis (ordinate). Of course, once a graph is set up, you may happen to know $y$

and not *x*. In that case, you can read the graph "backward," starting with *y* and finding the value of *x* that intersects with it on the line.

Some of the lines you encounter in graphs will be straight ones, but most of them will be curves representing formulas other than $y = a + bx$, the formula for a straight line. Any formula, however, no matter how complex it is, can be plotted on a graph as long as you know (or can assume) values of the constants (such as *a* or *b*). Changes in the constants merely alter the slope of the line or the point at which it intersects the ordinate. For example, in the equation $y = a + bx$, changing the value of *b* from ½ to 2 makes *y* grow four times as rapidly with respect to *x* as it did before; the line now moves upward at a steeper slope. Changing *a*, however, alters the point at which the line intercepts the *y* axis. When *a* is 1, this point is 1; when it is 2, it is 2, and so on.

A graph expresses a set of calculations from some particular formula. It is exceedingly handy because, once you have the graph, you don't need to make a new calculation for every change in one of the variables. All you have to do is read the answer off the graph. For this reason, many data and exact functions are presented to you in graphical form as well as in formulas. By using the graph, you can get around a lot of needless work. Graphs are therefore an aid in doing calculations. It will frequently pay you to make up your own graphs when you have a series of calculations to do based on one equation.

**Tables.** A table can be used to present the same kind of information a graph does but in different form. It gives the information to you in numbers rather than in lines. For that reason, it is more accurate than a graph. A graph usually can't be read to more than two significant figures, but you can put as many significant

## READING A TABLE

*Value of* y *for different values of* x *in different equations.*

| | $y = a + bx$ | | | |
| x | a = 2; b = ½ | a = 3; b = ⅓ | $y = x^2$ | $y = \log x$ |
|---|---|---|---|---|
| 0.00 | 2.00 | 3.00 | 0.00 | $-\infty$ |
| 1.00 | 2.50 | 3.33 | 1.00 | 0.000 |
| 2.00 | 3.00 | 3.67 | 4.00 | 0.301 |
| 3.00 | 3.50 | 4.00 | 9.00 | 0.477 |
| 4.00 | 4.00 | 4.33 | 16.00 | 0.602 |
| 5.00 | 4.50 | 4.67 | 25.00 | 0.699 |
| 6.00 | 5.00 | 5.00 | 36.00 | 0.778 |
| 7.00 | 5.50 | 5.33 | 49.00 | 0.845 |
| 8.00 | 6.00 | 5.67 | 64.00 | 0.903 |
| 9.00 | 6.50 | 6.00 | 81.00 | 0.954 |
| 10.00 | 7.00 | 6.33 | 100.00 | 1.000 |
| 11.00 | 7.50 | 6.67 | 121.00 | 1.041 |
| 12.00 | 8.00 | 7.00 | 144.00 | 1.079 |
| 13.00 | 8.50 | 7.33 | 169.00 | 1.114 |
| 14.00 | 9.00 | 7.67 | 196.00 | 1.146 |
| 15.00 | 9.50 | 8.00 | 225.00 | 1.176 |
| 16.00 | 10.00 | 8.33 | 256.00 | 1.204 |

figures as you wish (assuming you have them) in a table. That is one of the reasons why tables are sometimes used instead of graphs.

Notice another thing about a table. The left-hand column is usually a set of values for the independent variable $x$, the same variable plotted on the abscissa of a graph. Then each succeeding column, reading toward the right, represents the $y$ values corresponding to $x$. From one column to another, only the constants in the equation may change; or the nature of the equation may be changed. In the sample table nearby, the first $y$ column is a set of figures for $y = a + bx$, where $a = 2$ and $b = \frac{1}{2}$, the same value of constants we used in illustrating graphs. In the second column, the constants have been changed to $a = 3$ and $b = \frac{1}{3}$. In the third column, we have given values of $y$ when $y = x^2$; and in the last column, we have given the logarithm of $x$, the value of $y$ in $10^y = x$, or $y = \log x$. These are just examples, for we could put in the table any set of numbers for any formula representing the relation between $y$ and $x$.

Notice that a table gives discrete, not continuous, numbers. It gives only certain values of $y$ for certain values of $x$. A graph, on the other hand, may be continuous, for you can read any value of $y$ from any value of $x$—any that fits on the graph. So the graph is much better for solving a set of calculations for any and all values of two variables. On the other hand, the table is more accurate; it'll let you have any degree of precision you want. And when there are only a certain few values you may use the table for anyway, a table is better than a graph.

Tables also have a couple of other advantages. You can use them when the several lines they represent are so mixed up, overlapping, and intertwining that you couldn't read them in graphical form. Similarly, you can use them when the magnitudes of different sets of numbers are so different you couldn't show them conveniently on the same graph. Of course, you can also put in tables information you can't plot on graphs, such as a series of constants for different substances or other things that are not represented by equations.

To use tables and graphs effectively, you'll have to practice using the ones that you need for your particular purposes. If you have relatively little to do with numbers and mathematical problems, you may never need any more than a log table, a square-root table, an interest table (if you save or borrow money), a premium table (for insurance), and an annuity table (for your retirement plan). Textbooks in many subjects, however, employ tables and graphs to present principles and factual information. You must therefore be able to read them without difficulty. If you're a science or engineering student, you'll have a lot more use for tables and graphs. You'll probably want to purchase a book of mathematical tables and a handbook or two giving data, formulas, and constants important in your particular field.

TEN

# GETTING HELP

# AND BEING HELPFUL

THIS IS a do-it-yourself book, intended to show you how you can help yourself become a better student. We have concentrated on the more formal aspects of college study—using textbooks, taking notes in class, and taking examinations. In addition, however, most students sometimes get help from other sources, such as outlines, special files of old examinations, and various people like advisors and deans. These are the things we are going to discuss briefly in this chapter.

## BEYOND TEXTBOOKS

When you are learning a new subject, there are a lot of things besides lectures and textbooks that can help you. We will say a word or two about some of these things, specifically about workbooks, outlines, fraternity files, and outside readings. We'll try to tell you when these

things are going to be useful and what their limitations are.

**Workbooks and outlines.** In most college bookstores you will find some paperback books with titles such as *Outline of Chemistry, Outline of European History*, and so on. One or more "outlines" are published for each regular introductory course and some for more advanced courses. These outlines are just what their name implies; they give the bare essentials without extended explanations, illustrations, or details.

These outlines are useful, but they have limitations. They help a student see the fundamentals of a given subject, and they are likely to be of help in reviewing. On the other hand, some courses are not standardized, and the outlines are not likely to be a reliable guide to the subject matter of your particular course. Therefore, you can't follow them blindly.

Perhaps one of the best uses of outlines is for review of a more elementary subject. Suppose you are taking physics and you run into trouble with mathematics. An outline of high-school algebra will probably be quite useful to you.

Something more generally useful are the student workbooks, or manuals, written specifically to go along with some of your textbooks. These workbooks often accompany textbooks in introductory courses. They are designed to help you study your specific textbook. Content varies, but typically they include special projects and exercises to illustrate and explain the book, review questions, and sometimes self-test items that provide practice for examinations. In any case, the author who prepares the workbook strives to give you devices for becoming interested in and effectively studying the subject.

Sometimes your instructor will require the workbook; in other cases, he'll recommend it but not require it; or he may say little or nothing about it. No matter what he does, you will be wise to find out if there is a workbook that accompanies your textbook. (The preface will usually say whether a workbook or manual is available.) If you can, examine a copy of the workbook to determine whether it is likely to help you. Almost all workbooks are of some value, and some will help you enormously.

**Outside readings.** Textbooks and workbooks usually provide the core of reading for most courses. In many cases, however, instructors assign outside readings; and even if a particular instructor doesn't assign them, he is likely to recommend them; in any event, nearly every textbook will have lists of general references at the end of each chapter.

How valuable are these outside readings? Should you bother with them? Many, perhaps most, students don't unless they are required to do so. The fact is, though, that it is things like outside readings that give a genuine depth to your education.

In the first place, outside readings can and do help you better understand your basic textbook. They tell you about things missed in the textbook, and they sometimes give you a sufficiently different slant on some difficult topic so that you can understand it more easily. More than this, though, outside readings can add satisfaction to your study and arouse new curiosity in you.

In some subjects, particularly those in the humanities, outside readings provide the real meat of learning. The textbook is frequently just a skeleton on which the instructor hangs the body of the reading. To read about Plato in a textbook on the history of philosophy is only an introduction to reading Plato himself.

Finally, outside readings give you guidance in things you wish to study on your own. If you are undecided about whether you want to major in a particular subject or not, frequently a very little time spent skimming through some of the general references given in an introductory textbook will tell you whether you should go ahead with your plans or not.

Another kind of outside reading ought to be mentioned: journals and magazines in the general field of study. Many of these make interesting and educational reading. Sometimes they provide information and understanding of direct value in a course, but they are sure to make your formal studies more interesting and meaningful, in this way providing motivation and satisfaction in study. For example, if your major interests are in business and economics, there are the *Wall Street Journal, Barron's,* and *Business Week.* For the student of physics, there is *Physics Today*; for the general student of science, *Scientific Monthly,* or *Scientific American*; for the student of history, *American Heritage.* These are just a few examples that by no means exhaust the list. Some can be obtained on newsstands or in your bookstore. The rest are probably in your college library.

**Text films.** Motion pictures are being used more and more as teaching aids in the classroom, and you'll probably find that some will be shown in courses you take. Motion pictures can be extremely effective aids in learning, for they not only combine the best features of a teacher's explanation with the visual materials of a textbook but also can present experiments, demonstrations, and real events that otherwise are not feasible to bring into the classroom. For that reason, more and better teaching films are being produced each year, and they are gradually assuming a more important role in classroom teaching.

Because you are accustomed to being more entertained than taught by motion pictures, you probably tend to sit back and relax when a film is shown in the classroom. At least, we've seen a lot of students do this. If you are to learn from films, though, you have to regard them as something to be studied as carefully as your textbook or your class notes. In fact, since it is frequently possible to pack much more information and explanation into a motion picture than can be done in a comparable amount of talking or reading, you must really be on your toes to get the most from a film.

Films, like other things, ought to be surveyed before they are watched. You, of course, can't do this yourself, but the instructor usually does. Before he shows the film, he'll usually tell you what it is about and why he is showing it. Take notes on his explanation as you would on the survey he gives of what he is going to say in a lecture. Furthermore, you'll find that most teaching films have their own survey at the beginning.

Ideally, you should take notes fast and furiously while a film is being shown. In practice, however, you can't always do that because you may not be able to see what you're writing. (This is the chief disadvantage of films.) If the lighting is such that you can take notes, by all means do so; if not, try to make notes "in your head." Recite to yourself the important points during the course of the film. Then, as soon as the film is over, jot down rapidly all you can remember from it.

One word of warning. Because films are pictorial and make considerable use of everyday situations, you may have the impression that there isn't much that is "technical" or specific to take notes on. This is usually an illusion, however, for teaching films actually make definite points. You needn't remember every detail of each illustration, just as you don't take notes on all the illustrations an author uses in a textbook, but you should keep looking for main ideas and important details—as in reading textbooks—and write them down at the first opportunity. Because things move so fast in a film, it is even more important to review and recite what is covered as soon as it is over than it is to review lecture notes and textbook notes.

**Fraternity files.** To some fraternity members, the most frequented library and the most familiar outside reading is that wonderful collec-tion known as the "fraternity files." Dormitories and student cooperatives have files too. As a matter of fact, the existence of these files is so widespread that many colleges and individual instructors have arranged for files of old exams to be deposited in the college library so that they are available to all students. Old examinations are probably the most treasured items in such collections, but old outlines and course notes, themes and term papers, and almost anything may be in them.

There are few things in this world that are either all good or all bad, and this is true of fraternity files. Some good things can be said about them. They may help you, when you are studying for an examination, to get a good idea about what the examination will be like and to look over the sorts of items that can be expected. It is often useful too to look at other people's course notes to see how they have organized the material and what they found important enough to write down. If a student has been absent from class, he needs to consult such notes to fill in what he's missed. And in getting ideas for papers and the way they should be written, you will find it helpful to see samples of what others have done in the past.

In so far as such files serve these purposes, they are of value to the student. In practice, though, they can't really do these things very well. For one thing, they're "old." They have in them what happened last term, last year, or even some years back. Occasionally there's an instructor who hasn't changed his textbook, his lectures, or possibly his examinations for some time, but in most courses the outlines and lectures undergo some change, textbooks change periodically, and even if all these things are not too different, the examinations change. Almost any instructor using objective questions has a system for devising new questions and "rotating" old ones so that no two exams ever contain more than a small percentage of the same questions. Sometimes, in essay examinations, an instructor has some pet questions or old chestnuts that tend to pop up repeatedly, but he usually has some new ones too. Even his old ones may be rephrased enough to call for rather different answers even if, superficially, they seem to be the same as before.

What all this means is that you can waste your time with files of old examinations unless you know how to use them properly. One thing not to do with them is to use them to predict what you will get on an exam. Undoubtedly you will have a few lucky hits, but the chances are that for every such hit you will be misled into not studying something which didn't appear on one of the old exams.

The fact that fraternity files are old and that courses change also applies to using old course notes and outlines. Most instructors continually alter their courses in many little ways (even if the courses do not have new instructors). When you rely too much on old course notes, you don't know how much you are missing of what is current in the course. The only way in which old course notes and outlines are useful is when they are placed side by side with a good set of notes on the course as it is currently being given. Even here, they are apt to be rather dangerous if there has been a radical change in viewpoint or method in teaching a particular course.

Another thing wrong with unofficial course files is that they are of unknown quality. You don't really know how good the material is that you're studying. Furthermore, even if you have some idea of the quality, from marks on the examinations or term papers, you don't know how relevant the material will be for what you want. In the case of class notes, you really have no way at all of knowing how good the notes are.

Probably the worst thing about fraternity files is that they encourage poor study habits. They give you a false sense of security, and they encourage piecemeal and disorganized study. Files of old examinations can be somewhat useful to you if you approach them the right way. Don't rely blindly on your ability to memorize individual questions, but instead try using old examinations as self-testing devices. You can get a rough idea of how much you know about a particular subject by taking one of the old

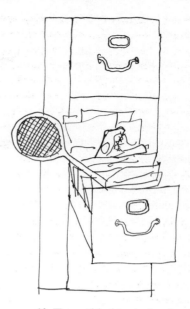

examinations yourself. Even this has to be done judiciously, for it can lead you to emphasize the wrong things.

To a lesser extent, old papers and notes are useful for the same purpose. If you look at old term papers, look especially at the kinds of correction the instructor has made. You may be able to avoid mistakes in form and style this way. But above all, do not use old papers and lab reports for copying. This is the surest way to misunderstand the content of a course. Sooner or later the instructor is going to find out that you really don't understand and that you have been blindly copying somebody else's work, and then you will be in trouble.

All this adds up to a warning not to rely too heavily on files. They may be useful if you approach them with the idea of actually doing some work and not just using them as a crutch, but don't depend on them to take the place of good techniques of study.

## GETTING HELP

There are times when every student needs help from other people. The good student is self-reliant, but in order to plan his program and to know what to study and what is expected of him, he needs help from other people. We'll discuss the matter of getting help very briefly in this section.

**Other students.** Students help each other in a number of ways. You can pick up a good deal of information about particular courses from other students. Sometimes this information is valuable. You should take it, though, with a grain of salt. The judgment of students is not infallible, and things change from time to time. Be prepared to make your own assessment of a course and your own decisions about handling the work in it.

Students who are taking a course together should also occasionally compare notes. In this way you can exchange ideas on class notes and check with one another on important and difficult points.

Studying with other students for an examination can be valuable if done properly. Don't rely on other students as your sole or principal preparation for examinations. Before you go into a session with other students, you should have studied the material thoroughly by yourself. A session with other students should serve only as a review and checkout for what you've already studied.

Group studying does one important thing: It provides a good opportunity for oral recitation. This is the most valuable aspect of group studying. But, in addition, it allows you to correct one another, and it gives you a better prediction of what an examination will be like.

To be effective, such groups should be run in an orderly fashion. When the group first meets, it ought to discuss its plan of action and set up an agenda much as any other conference would. Then you can take turns giving oral summaries of important points.

Don't get bogged down arguing about little points. And, above all, don't take on faith what another student says about something. He can be wrong. Make a habit of checking anything new that you hear from another student.

Aside from studying together for examinations, there are, of course, other times when students can help each other. If there is something in a course you don't understand and

you know another student who clearly understands the particular point, you can ask him to explain it to you. It will pay you, in fact, to keep tabs both on your weak points and on the abilities of other students so that you know when and to whom to go for help. If, on the other hand, someone asks you for help on a point, you should be willing within limits to give him some time. Besides being the friendly thing to do, assisting other people can help you because it gives you a chance to recite what you know. Consequently you'll remember and understand better the points you've helped others with. (It's an axiom among teachers that there is no better way to learn a subject than to teach it to somebody else.)

**Instructors.** Instructors can help you in ways other than in classes. The most important thing about getting help from your instructor is not to ask him for help with anything you should have gotten yourself. If you've been cutting class or been going to sleep, don't ask him to tell you what you should have heard if you had been listening. This will leave an unfavorable impression with the instructor, and it is impolite and unfair. If you miss something, try to recoup your loss by asking your fellow students about what you have missed.

Avoid asking your instructor for unreasonable or special favors. Don't, for example, ask to borrow his notes. This kind of request will merely annoy him. Incidentally, under the heading of unreasonable or special favors usually comes the request to take an examination late. There are few things which impress an instructor more unfavorably than such a request, and you will be wise to avoid it unless absolutely necessary.

As examination time draws near, students ask all sorts of questions about what will be on the examination. One of the silliest questions, often heard, is "How much are we supposed to know?" The answer, of course, is "As much as possible." It is more reasonable to ask specific questions about your responsibilities for an examination. You might, for example, ask, "Are we responsible for all the names of people mentioned in the textbook?" Or "How much stress will be placed on dates?" (Or derivations, formulas, experiments, and so on.) The instructor is usually willing to tell you his general policy on such matters. You will surely want to know what kind of examination to expect; if the instructor doesn't tell you, ask.

Instructors have a limited amount of time. Therefore you ought to try to get help from your instructors immediately before or after the regularly scheduled class hours. Be brief and businesslike.

Don't let this advice, however, discourage you from raising legitimate and interesting questions with your instructor. If there is an important point he hasn't made clear or something you just don't understand, don't hesitate to ask him to straighten you out. Don't shy away, either, from asking questions that interest you or questions about the implications of the things you learn in a course. Instructors like to have interested students, and they particularly like to see students with an inquisitive bent who learn more than is required and who want to understand the meaning of things they learn. If you choose a convenient time and avoid pestering your instructor with picayune questions, you can benefit immensely from discussions with him. He, on the other hand, is pretty sure to enjoy and to profit from your genuine expression of interest in his course.

**Faculty advisors.** In many colleges, each student is assigned to a faculty advisor. His responsibilities vary from one college to another. In general, however, the advisor's duty is to help the student with decisions about course programs and with any special academic problems that come up. How well this relationship works out in practice depends both on the student and on the advisor.

First of all, do for yourself all that you can do. You must read your college catalogue to see what courses are offered, consult schedules to see which courses conflict with each other and hence cannot fit into your schedule, and do the arithmetic involved in determining how many "credits" you should take or are planning to take in any particular term. In so far as you are sure what you are going to do, you should make out yourself the forms required for the advisor's approval or action. In general, go to your advisor only after you have thoroughly studied your own problems, learned all you can about them, and have specific questions well formulated.

Remember, too, that an advisor's job is to advise and not to make your decisions for you. He'll give you information you can't get yourself as well as opinions based on what he knows about courses and their value for your objectives. In the end, though, the choices to be made among electives and different arrangements of courses are up to you. You shouldn't want to be told what to do, nor should you ask your advisor to decide matters of individual interest, taste, or preference.

Students often have personal problems that may, within reason, be taken to the advisor. If you are failing or doing poorly in any of your courses, if you have trouble studying (which you shouldn't after you've read this book), or even if personal worries or difficulties seriously hamper your work, you should be able to present these problems to your advisor for some help and guidance. Don't expect too much, though, or take too much of his time. If you state your problem clearly, he may be able to give you some helpful hints, but he can seldom solve your problem for you. That's something only you can do. Moreover, if you have serious personal and emotional problems, the typical faculty advisor has neither the time nor training to do much about them. About the most he can do is to send you to a counselor or someone else professionally trained to deal with such problems.

**Help from special sources.** Sometimes students need help from special sources. You may need some remedial work to make up serious deficiencies in basic skills like arithmetic or reading. Or you may need some personal counseling and advice. In these and other cases, you will usually find that there are people at your institution specifically designated to help you. It is a very good idea to find out what kinds of special service are available to you in the way of counseling, study clinics, and so on, and make use of them if you have the need. These services exist because college administrators are convinced that far more students fall by the wayside than is necessary. We know that these special services help keep some students in good standing in college who would otherwise leave or flunk out. If you are in trouble, by all means find out what services are available to you.

**When you're in trouble.**  We are sure that much we've said in this book will help you stay out of trouble as far as your studies are concerned. You may have gotten the book too late to help you much with the troubles you already have. Or you may find yourself in some kind of difficulty despite all your best efforts. Certainly it is the exceptional and lucky student who can escape ever having any bad moments in college. So in addition to all the things we've said up to now, we have a few points of specific advice about what to do when you find yourself in any one of the troubles that are typical of college students.

Suppose you've been working hard at a course, doing all you know how to do, and yet you just can't seem to master it. You're doing poor work, falling behind, not understanding the subject, and find it over your head. What do you do?

If this is the case, you should, first of all, try to diagnose it as early as possible. Don't drift along hoping for the best any longer than it takes you to tell that something is wrong. Don't wait for a failing mark on an hour exam to demonstrate what you had good reason to suspect before the exam. When you've got a good idea you're in trouble, try to do something about it.

To do anything, you'll have to figure out, at least roughly, what the trouble really is. Are you inadequately prepared for the course? Is there some one thing about the course that seems particularly wrong? Does its special vocab-

ulary give you trouble? Do you have difficulty with calculations, problems, or laboratory work? Ask yourself questions like these to formulate as well as you can what may be wrong.

Your next problem is to decide whether you can do something to remedy your difficulties or whether you must consider dropping the course. At this point, your instructor may help you. If you go to him prepared to tell him what your particular problems are, he may be able to tell you the steps you should take to get straightened out. He may be able to spot something you're doing consistently wrong. He may discover a weakness in your preparation and prescribe some reading or special exercises that will help you. On the other hand, he may find that you've simply gotten into a course that is too difficult for you—this can easily happen, for example, when students continue a foreign language they've previously had in high school—and suggest some other course that is better for a student with your background.

If you realize your trouble and seek help early enough in a course, you usually can work out some wise course of action. If you can improve, you can find out how. If you aren't likely to, there is still time to drop the course and rearrange your program without undue hardship. It's usually not a good idea, though, to drop a course impulsively and without seeking competent advice, especially if the course is one that is required or recommended for your field of study. For this reason, many colleges require the approval of both the instructor and faculty advisor for the dropping of a course—not as a matter of red tape but to encourage the student to seek their help in deciding whether it is a wise thing to do. In any case, it is a good idea to get the advice of your instructor and faculty advisor before dropping a course because you find it giving you trouble.

You don't have to be in serious trouble or on the verge of dropping a course to seek some substantial help in it. Even good students find there are often some aspects of a course they have trouble handling. If they make a list of the things that bother them and then arrange with the instructor for a few minutes of his time, they often can run down the list and get a few pointers to straighten themselves out.

Suppose now that you get pretty well along in a course with an hour exam or two behind you and find that you are doing unsatisfactory work. It's probably too late to drop the course without some sort of penalty. What we've said throughout this book about learning from one's mistakes and poor grades is particularly appropriate here. Instead of quibbling about your grade and then putting aside the paper that received the grade, it's time to find out specifically what's wrong. If you can, you might go over your paper with another, better student to see if you can learn anything that way. If you're still not satisfied that you know where your shortcomings are, ask your instructor to go over it with you. If you are really interested in improving, instructors are almost always willing to take a little time to show you exactly what you did wrong and what you should have done to do it right.

Sometimes things get to such a point that you have little hope of pulling yourself out of a hole. You've done poor work all term and then, at the end, are still doing poorly. In this situation, it may be too late to raise your grade, but it's not too late to learn something that will help you avoid similar difficulties in the future. Far too many students who have received a final grade in a course don't bother to collect papers they could obtain from their instructor to see why they did badly. In many cases, they should ask to go over the paper with the instructor, not with any thought of getting their grade changed but with the idea of pinpointing their own weaknesses and mistakes. If they did this, they might get off to a good start in the next term and not get into trouble again.

Sometimes the trouble may lie not in mistakes or doing things that can be corrected but rather in something more deeply rooted. The student may be in personal difficulties with other people, worrying too much about non-academic things, and generally not able to ap-

ply himself the way he knows he should. If that's the trouble, it's not one for the instructor to handle. Rather it's time to take advantage of some of the special services we mentioned above and particularly of the services of a psychological counselor. If you feel deeply depressed, terribly anxious, or are forever getting into social difficulties, you ought to go to such a counselor without delay or, if such a counselor isn't available, to a psychiatrist. There is no point in jeopardizing your academic work and your own happiness. If you're in emotional trouble, go immediately to someone professionally competent to help you.

We'll mention finally the possibility of trouble arising because you're a "round peg in a square hole." You may be attempting to take a course of study in which you aren't really interested. There may be another set of courses in which you will be more interested and more capable. You may, similarly, be shooting for a vocational objective for which you are not suited. As a consequence, you may be so poorly motivated that you simply can't muster the effort to do the sort of work you know you should. Again, this is a situation for professional help; seek out a psychologist, vocational counselor, or someone equipped to help you find the vocational objective and course of studies for which you are best suited.

## STUDENT MANNERS

In winding up this book on how to study, we should say a few things about student manners. These have a bearing on your academic success as well as on your personal relations with your instructors and fellow students.

**Classroom behavior.** Get to class on time. In addition to the things that you miss by coming to class late, late arrivals disturb other students and the instructor. Once in class, carry your share of class activities and be a good listener. If the class is a discussion class it is to your advantage to take part in the discussion. This is the way you will learn, and in some cases instructors are apt to judge you by the degree to which you participate. If your class is a lecture class, be an attentive and a polite listener. Whether you realize it or not, the instructor is usually very sensitive to the demeanor of a class; a roomful of students sprawled out, half asleep, is not an inspiring sight and lowers the lecturer's morale. Finally, don't jump the gun at the end of the hour. Wait until the instructor is through before snapping your notebook shut and gathering up your books.

A really basic point about your relationships with your instructors is to do your work on time. To be late with daily assignments, term papers, and similar kinds of work is a sign of bad management on your part. Some instructors justifiably penalize students for being late, but even if you aren't penalized, it is grossly unfair and a reflection on you not to be on time.

**Conferences.** As we've pointed out above, students have occasions for seeking conferences with instructors, and instructors consider consultation with students a part of their job as teachers. You should remember, though, that their time is valuable. Besides classroom teaching and preparation for classes, faculty members have hundreds of things to do: a lot of reading to stay on their toes as teachers, professional meetings to go to, letters and recommendations to write, committee meetings to attend, and many miscellaneous chores connected with the running of the college. In some institutions, research is a substantial part of teachers' work.

What all this means is that you should try not to waste an instructor's time. If your question is a brief one, don't run him down in his office and interrupt him there; try to catch him just before or after class when he can handle it quickly. Don't ask him silly questions or questions you should figure out for yourself. Don't ask him to do what you, as a self-respecting young adult, should be able to do for yourself. Where papers or recommendations are concerned, make them out as fully in advance as

possible. Even little things like writing in your name or addressing an envelope are time-consuming and annoying. If you can do them, don't ask him to.

If your problem really requires a conference lasting several minutes, don't just "drop in" on the instructor unless he has previously told you to or posts office hours. Ask him for an appointment, stating your business when you ask for it. Once the appointment is made, by all means *keep it*. Later on in life, you'll have to keep your appointments punctually, and college is none too early to learn such considerate and businesslike habits.

When you get to a conference, be prepared to state your problem succinctly and clearly. Don't fumble and stumble, doing the thinking you should have done before you came. Stay on the subject of your business; when your business is finished, exchange an amenity or two and be on your way. If you can't tell when you're finished, be sensitive to the signals in the situation. If the instructor gets fidgety, leans forward in his chair, stands up, or provides some other hint that the end has come, close things up promptly.

If you manage your conferences with your instructor in a businesslike way, he'll have a much better impression of you, which may come in good stead when the time arrives to write a letter of recommendation for you. More important, he'll think more kindly of students in general and be more inclined to be helpful. And he'll have more time to do the things he needs to do to be an effective teacher and scholar.

Students seldom mean to be unmannerly in class or to impose on the instructor. They're often just thoughtless or impatient. These brief comments about student manners are intended simply as a reminder of some of the things you can do to help make studying and teaching a little easier—for both your fellow students and your teachers.

## OTHER BOOKS ON READING AND STUDY

Armstrong, W. H.: *Study Is Hard Work*, Harper, New York, 1956.

Bennett, M. E.: *College and Life*, 3d ed., McGraw-Hill, New York, 1952.

Bird, C., and D. M. Bird: *Learning More by Effective Study*, Appleton-Century-Crofts, New York, 1945.

Bull, W. E., and L. E. Drake: *Aids to Language Learning: Spanish*, College Typing Co., Madison, Wis., 1941.

Eells, H.: *How to Write a Term Paper*, Edwards, Ann Arbor, Mich., 1931.

Good, W. R.: *How to Prepare a Term Report*, Alumni Press, Ann Arbor, Mich., 1932.

Harris, A. J.: *How to Increase Reading Ability*, Longmans, New York, 1949.

Lewis, N.: *How to Read Better and Faster*, Crowell, New York, 1944.

McCallister, J. M.: *Purposeful Reading in College*, Appleton-Century-Crofts, New York, 1942.

McKown, H. C.: *How to Pass a Written Examination*, McGraw-Hill, New York, 1943.

Moore, H.: *A Practice Manual in Vocabulary Building*, Psychological Corporation, New York, 1941.

Orchard, N. E.: *Study Successfully: 18 Keys to Better Work*, McGraw-Hill, New York, 1953.

Robinson, F. P.: *Effective Study*, Harper, New York, 1946.

Schreve, F.: *Psychology of the Teaching of English*, Christopher Publishing Co., Boston, 1941.

Witty, P.: *How to Become a Better Reader*, Science Research, Chicago, 1953.

# INDEX

# PROVISIONAL WORKING SCHEDULE

| Time | Monday | Tuesday | Wednesday | Thursday | Friday | Saturday | Sunday |
|---|---|---|---|---|---|---|---|
| 8:00 | | | | | | | |
| 8:30 | | | | | | | |
| 9:00 | | | | | | | |
| 9:30 | | | | | | | |
| 10:00 | | | | | | | |
| 10:30 | | | | | | | |
| 11:00 | | | | | | | |
| 11:30 | | | | | | | |
| 12:00 | | | | | | | |
| 12:30 | | | | | | | |
| 1:00 | | | | | | | |
| 1:30 | | | | | | | |
| 2:00 | | | | | | | |
| 2:30 | | | | | | | |
| 3:00 | | | | | | | |
| 3:30 | | | | | | | |
| 4:00 | | | | | | | |
| 4.30 | | | | | | | |
| 5:00 | | | | | | | |
| 5:30 | | | | | | | |
| 6:00 | | | | | | | |
| 6:30 | | | | | | | |
| 7:00 | | | | | | | |
| 7:30 | | | | | | | |
| 8:00 | | | | | | | |
| 8:30 | | | | | | | |
| 9:00 | | | | | | | |
| 9:30 | | | | | | | |
| 10:00 | | | | | | | |

# PROVISIONAL WORKING SCHEDULE

| Time | Monday | Tuesday | Wednesday | Thursday | Friday | Saturday | Sunday |
|------|--------|---------|-----------|----------|--------|----------|--------|
| 8:00 | | | | | | | |
| 8:30 | | | | | | | |
| 9:00 | | | | | | | |
| 9:30 | | | | | | | |
| 10:00 | | | | | | | |
| 10:30 | | | | | | | |
| 11:00 | | | | | | | |
| 11:30 | | | | | | | |
| 12:00 | | | | | | | |
| 12:30 | | | | | | | |
| 1:00 | | | | | | | |
| 1:30 | | | | | | | |
| 2:00 | | | | | | | |
| 2:30 | | | | | | | |
| 3:00 | | | | | | | |
| 3:30 | | | | | | | |
| 4:00 | | | | | | | |
| 4.30 | | | | | | | |
| 5:00 | | | | | | | |
| 5:30 | | | | | | | |
| 6:00 | | | | | | | |
| 6:30 | | | | | | | |
| 7:00 | | | | | | | |
| 7:30 | | | | | | | |
| 8:00 | | | | | | | |
| 8:30 | | | | | | | |
| 9:00 | | | | | | | |
| 9:30 | | | | | | | |
| 10:00 | | | | | | | |

# PROVISIONAL WORKING SCHEDULE

| Time | Monday | Tuesday | Wednesday | Thursday | Friday | Saturday | Sunday |
|------|--------|---------|-----------|----------|--------|----------|--------|
| 8:00 | | | | | | | |
| 8:30 | | | | | | | |
| 9:00 | | | | | | | |
| 9:30 | | | | | | | |
| 10:00 | | | | | | | |
| 10:30 | | | | | | | |
| 11:00 | | | | | | | |
| 11:30 | | | | | | | |
| 12:00 | | | | | | | |
| 12:30 | | | | | | | |
| 1:00 | | | | | | | |
| 1:30 | | | | | | | |
| 2:00 | | | | | | | |
| 2:30 | | | | | | | |
| 3:00 | | | | | | | |
| 3:30 | | | | | | | |
| 4:00 | | | | | | | |
| 4.30 | | | | | | | |
| 5:00 | | | | | | | |
| 5:30 | | | | | | | |
| 6:00 | | | | | | | |
| 6:30 | | | | | | | |
| 7:00 | | | | | | | |
| 7:30 | | | | | | | |
| 8:00 | | | | | | | |
| 8:30 | | | | | | | |
| 9:00 | | | | | | | |
| 9:30 | | | | | | | |
| 10:00 | | | | | | | |

# PROVISIONAL WORKING SCHEDULE

| Time | Monday | Tuesday | Wednesday | Thursday | Friday | Saturday | Sunday |
|------|--------|---------|-----------|----------|--------|----------|--------|
| 8:00 | | | | | | | |
| 8:30 | | | | | | | |
| 9:00 | | | | | | | |
| 9:30 | | | | | | | |
| 10:00 | | | | | | | |
| 10:30 | | | | | | | |
| 11:00 | | | | | | | |
| 11:30 | | | | | | | |
| 12:00 | | | | | | | |
| 12:30 | | | | | | | |
| 1:00 | | | | | | | |
| 1:30 | | | | | | | |
| 2:00 | | | | | | | |
| 2:30 | | | | | | | |
| 3:00 | | | | | | | |
| 3:30 | | | | | | | |
| 4:00 | | | | | | | |
| 4.30 | | | | | | | |
| 5:00 | | | | | | | |
| 5:30 | | | | | | | |
| 6:00 | | | | | | | |
| 6:30 | | | | | | | |
| 7:00 | | | | | | | |
| 7:30 | | | | | | | |
| 8:00 | | | | | | | |
| 8:30 | | | | | | | |
| 9:00 | | | | | | | |
| 9:30 | | | | | | | |
| 10:00 | | | | | | | |

# FINAL WORKING SCHEDULE

| Time | Monday | Tuesday | Wednesday | Thursday | Friday | Saturday | Sunday |
|---|---|---|---|---|---|---|---|
| 8:00 | | | | | | | |
| 8:30 | | | | | | | |
| 9:00 | | | | | | | |
| 9:30 | | | | | | | |
| 10:00 | | | | | | | |
| 10:30 | | | | | | | |
| 11:00 | | | | | | | |
| 11:30 | | | | | | | |
| 12:00 | | | | | | | |
| 12:30 | | | | | | | |
| 1:00 | | | | | | | |
| 1:30 | | | | | | | |
| 2:00 | | | | | | | |
| 2:30 | | | | | | | |
| 3:00 | | | | | | | |
| 3:30 | | | | | | | |
| 4:00 | | | | | | | |
| 4:30 | | | | | | | |
| 5:00 | | | | | | | |
| 5:30 | | | | | | | |
| 6:00 | | | | | | | |
| 6:30 | | | | | | | |
| 7:00 | | | | | | | |
| 7:30 | | | | | | | |
| 8:00 | | | | | | | |
| 8:30 | | | | | | | |
| 9:00 | | | | | | | |
| 9:30 | | | | | | | |
| 10:00 | | | | | | | |

# WESTMAR COLLEGE LIBRARY

**FINAL WORKING SCHEDULE**

| Time | Monday | Tuesday | Wednesday | Thursday | Friday | Saturday | Sunday |
|------|--------|---------|-----------|----------|--------|----------|--------|
| 8:00 | | | | | | | |
| 8:30 | | | | | | | |
| 9:00 | | | | | | | |
| 9:30 | | | | | | | |
| 10:00 | | | | | | | |
| 10:30 | | | | | | | |
| 11:00 | | | | | | | |
| 11:30 | | | | | | | |
| 12:00 | | | | | | | |
| 12:30 | | | | | | | |
| 1:00 | | | | | | | |
| 1:30 | | | | | | | |
| 2:00 | | | | | | | |
| 2:30 | | | | | | | |
| 3:00 | | | | | | | |
| 3:30 | | | | | | | |
| 4:00 | | | | | | | |
| 4:30 | | | | | | | |
| 5:00 | | | | | | | |
| 5:30 | | | | | | | |
| 6:00 | | | | | | | |
| 6:30 | | | | | | | |
| 7:00 | | | | | | | |
| 7:30 | | | | | | | |
| 8:00 | | | | | | | |
| 8:30 | | | | | | | |
| 9:00 | | | | | | | |
| 9:30 | | | | | | | |
| 10:00 | | | | | | | |